Estate Planning for the Future: A Family Guide to Preserving Wealth and Legacy

Effortless Estate Strategies: Secure Your Future in 7 Easy Steps

Zachary G. Farris

© Copyright 2024 - All rights reserved.

The content contained within this book may not be reproduced, duplicated or transmitted without direct written permission from the author or the publisher.

Under no circumstances will any blame or legal responsibility be held against the publisher, or author, for any damages, reparation, or monetary loss due to the information contained within this book, either directly or indirectly.

Legal Notice:

This book is copyright protected. It is only for personal use. You cannot amend, distribute, sell, use, quote or paraphrase any part, or the content within this book, without the consent of the author or publisher.

Disclaimer Notice:

Please note the information contained within this document is for educational and entertainment purposes only. All effort has been executed to present accurate, up to date, reliable, complete information. No warranties of any kind are declared or implied. Readers acknowledge that the author is not engaged in the rendering of legal, financial, medical or professional advice. The content within this book has been derived from various sources. Please consult a licensed professional before attempting any techniques outlined in this book.

By reading this document, the reader agrees that under no circumstances is the author responsible for any losses, direct or indirect, that are incurred as a result of the use of the information contained within this document, including, but not limited to, errors, omissions, or inaccuracies.

Table of Contents

INTRODUCTION 1

CHAPTER 1: ESTATE PLANNING BASICS 3

UNDERSTANDING ESTATE PLANNING 3
    What Is Estate Planning and Why Should You Care? 3
    Common Misconceptions 4
    The Need for Estate Planning 5
KEY COMPONENTS OF ESTATE PLANNING 5
    Wills and Trusts 5
    Powers of Attorney 6
    Health Care Directives 6
    Beneficiary Designations 7
ESTATE PLANNING AND YOUR FAMILY 7
    Protecting Your Loved Ones 7
    Ensuring Financial Security 7
    Preserving Family Harmony 8

CHAPTER 2: ASSESSING YOUR ESTATE PLANNING NEEDS 9

PERSONAL AND FAMILY ASSESSMENT 9
    Identifying Assets and Liabilities 9
    Understanding Family Dynamics 11
    Future Goals and Aspirations 11
SPECIAL CONSIDERATIONS 11
    Blended Families 12
    Business Ownership 12
    Charitable Intentions 13
SETTING CLEAR OBJECTIVES 14
    Short-Term and Long-Term Goals 14
    Protecting Vulnerable Family Members 14
    Leaving a Lasting Legacy 15

CHAPTER 3: CRAFTING YOUR WILL 17

THE IMPORTANCE OF A WILL 17
    Legal Necessities 17
    Controlling Asset Distribution 18
    Minimizing Family Conflicts 18
WRITING YOUR WILL 18
    Choosing an Executor 19
    Detailing Asset Distribution 20
    Providing for Minors and Dependents 21
COMMON PITFALLS TO AVOID 21
    Vague Language 22
    Not Updating Regularly 23
    Overlooking Digital Assets 23

CHAPTER 4: UNDERSTANDING AND UTILIZING TRUSTS 25

TYPES OF TRUSTS 25
    Revocable vs. Irrevocable Trusts 26
    Special Needs Trusts 27

  Living Trusts 27
  Other Types of Trusts 27
 SETTING UP A TRUST 28
  Choosing a Trustee 29
  Trust Conditions and Clauses 29
  Funding the Trust 30
 BENEFITS OF TRUSTS 31
  Avoiding Probate 31
  Tax Advantages 32
  Long-Term Asset Management 32

CHAPTER 5: ADVANCED HEALTH CARE DIRECTIVES 33

 UNDERSTANDING HEALTH CARE DIRECTIVES 33
  Living Wills 34
  Healthcare Power of Attorney 34
  The Importance of Clarity 34
 CREATING YOUR DIRECTIVE 35
  Outlining Your Medical Wishes 35
  Choosing a Health Care Proxy 36
  Discussing with Family 37
 LEGAL AND ETHICAL CONSIDERATIONS 37
  State Laws and Regulations 37
  Ethical Dilemmas 38
  Ensuring Compliance 38

CHAPTER 6: FINANCIAL POWERS OF ATTORNEY 39

 THE ROLE OF FINANCIAL POWERS OF ATTORNEY 39
  Durable vs. Springing Powers 40
  Selecting an Agent 41
  Defining Scope and Authority 41
 SETTING UP YOUR POWER OF ATTORNEY 42
  Legal Requirements 42
  Communicating with Your Agent 43
  Incorporating into Your Estate Plan 43
 AVOIDING COMMON MISTAKES 43
  Overly Broad Powers 44
  Failing to Update 44
  Not Having Alternate Agents 44

CHAPTER 7: ASSET MANAGEMENT AND PROTECTION 47

 ASSESSING AND ORGANIZING ASSETS 47
  Inventory of Assets 47
  Valuation and Documentation 48
  Digital Asset Management 49
 PROTECTING YOUR ASSETS 49
  Insurance Strategies 49
  Liability Considerations 50
  Asset Protection Trusts 50
 DIGITAL ASSET, CRYPTOCURRENCY AND CYBER INSURANCE 51
  Inventory and Valuation 51
  Estate Planning for Cryptocurrency 52
  Cyber Insurance 52
 STRATEGIES FOR GROWTH AND PRESERVATION 52
  Investment Strategies 53
  Succession Planning 53
  Charitable Giving 54

CHAPTER 8: ESTATE PLANNING AND TAXES 55

ESTATE AND INHERITANCE TAXES 55
- *Federal and State Taxes* 55
- *Taxable Assets* 56
- *Minimizing Tax Burden* 57

TAX PLANNING STRATEGIES 57
- *Gifting Assets* 58
- *Trusts and Tax Implications* 58
- *Charitable Donations* 59

WORKING WITH TAX PROFESSIONALS 59
- *Finding the Right Advisor* 60
- *Regular Tax Reviews* 60
- *Staying Informed on Tax Laws* 60

CHAPTER 9: UPDATING AND MAINTAINING YOUR ESTATE PLAN 63

REVIEWING YOUR ESTATE PLAN 63
- *Regular Check-Ups* 63
- *Responding to Life Changes* 64
- *Legal Updates* 64

MAKING NECESSARY ADJUSTMENTS 65
- *Amending Documents* 65
- *Reassessing Goals and Needs* 65
- *Communicating Changes to Family* 66

ENSURING CONTINUOUS RELEVANCE 66
- *Long-Term Vision* 67
- *Adapting to New Circumstances* 67
- *Engaging with Professionals* 68

CHAPTER 10: LEGACY PLANNING AND FAMILY DYNAMICS 69

DEFINING YOUR LEGACY 69
- *Personal Values and Beliefs* 69
- *Family Traditions and Histories* 70
- *Community and Philanthropic Goals* 71

COMMUNICATING YOUR LEGACY 71
- *Family Meetings* 71
- *Ethical Wills* 72
- *Storytelling and Memory Sharing* 72

NAVIGATING FAMILY DYNAMICS 73
- *Addressing Conflicts* 73
- *Fairness vs. Equality* 74
- *Preparing the Next Generation* 74

BONUS CHAPTER: ESTATE PLANNING AS A LIFELONG PROCESS 75

THE EVOLVING NATURE OF ESTATE PLANNING 75
- *Life Stages and Estate Planning* 75
- *Adapting to Personal and Financial Growth* 76
- *Anticipating Future Needs* 76

CONTINUOUS EDUCATION AND AWARENESS 77
- *Keeping Informed on Legal Changes* 77
- *Staying Updated with Financial Trends* 77
- *Lifelong Learning in Estate Planning* 77

ENGAGING WITH ESTATE PLANNING COMMUNITIES 78
- *Joining Support Groups and Forums* 78
- *Attending Workshops and Seminars* 79
- *Networking with Professionals and Peers* 79

CONCLUSION	81
GLOSSARY	83
REFERENCES	87

Introduction

Do you feel stuck, have no clue about how to do estate planning, or even know what estate planning is?

More so because you are overwhelmed with a plethora of legal jargon and paperwork to fill out?

I know the feeling when I first dived into the world of estate planning. I was lost just like you are. I had no clue what I needed to do, and I was anxious since I had to make sure everything adhered to the law.

But just like you, I had the same genuine intention and that was to make sure I did my estate planning so that my children and grandchildren got whatever I made with my blood and sweat.

I wanted to pass my wealth down to them—and that it would be *guaranteed* even though I won't be alive to witness it.

I was emotionally touched by a sad experience faced by one of my close friends. He lost his father when he was in his early 20s. He was still hustling at that age—just completed college, had loads of student loan debt to be paid off, and still hunting for a job. Being the only child and needing to support his mourning mother, he had to inherit his father's estate.

Unfortunately, he learned that his father didn't leave a will behind and also he had a lot of debt. He experienced a court process called probate where his father's estate gets administered and settles who gets his assets.

Without having a personal representative with whom his family is familiar, the court ended up appointing an "administrator" to settle all estate-related affairs—because the deceased died without a will.

This turned out to be a horrible scenario for my friend. He was kept in the dark regarding what his father's estate consisted of, and everything revolved around creditors coming up to get paid from his father's estate.

Some relatives managed to inherit some of the deceased's assets and properties which should have been rightfully inherited by his son. The whole fiasco took months, and money, and entirely drained my friend and his mourning mother.

This was an experience that he had to suffer because his father didn't take his estate planning seriously and the state court ended up taking control of the deceased's asset distribution.

Many skip estate planning or don't do the whole thing properly because of several reasons. It can be because the entire approach seems like a lot of work for them so it gets put off regularly.

It could be because they feel too old and are more anxious about death, that they don't feel interested in planning their estate. It could be also because they don't want to bring up such a subject with their loved ones and communicate their estate plan.

If any of these reasons resonate with you, it's natural! It's all psychological friction that makes it difficult for us to take action and preserve our family's future and financial security.

Eventually, you are in control of your actions and made one by reading this book. I am here with a moral duty to help you understand how you can take those steps.

My name is Zachary Farris and with over 10 years of personal experience in providing life insurance for families, I understand the importance of planning generational wealth.

This book demystifies estate planning and provides a simple, actionable guide. This book aims to show you that estate planning can be effortless and empowering. This is communicated throughout the book with how it is structured—organized and simplified content.

You will find information simplified by focusing on the most important details, and walking through practical situations when doing estate planning and what happens after your death.

This guide is for those who are leaning into the waters of procrastination and putting off an important moral duty to preserve their assets and valuable belongings for their loved ones.

You will find this read to be simple and organized with the intention that you take easy and actionable steps towards actually doing your estate plan correctly and eliminating any fear of confusion and legal complications.

If you are ready to start your journey, take the first step and keep turning the pages to get wiser on this important subject.

Chapter 1:

Estate Planning Basics

Nearly 60% of people in the United States are unprepared for the inevitable and do not have any will or estate plan in place (*Will(ful) Neglect: Survey Reveals Nearly 60% of Americans Unprepared for the Inevitable,* 2023). As a result, these families experience conflicts after the passing of a family member.

We have already understood the common reasons why many—including yourself—tend to put off their estate planning. Most of these reasons are ultimately tied to one thing—education!

When you do estate planning, it requires a minimum foundational knowledge to get started and this is why this chapter will help you grasp the foundational elements of estate planning.

Let's learn more about the basics, shall we?

Understanding Estate Planning

What Is Estate Planning and Why Should You Care?

Let's begin with understanding what exactly estate planning is. For that, first, understand what an estate is. An estate is something of value that you own and can be passed down to your heirs, creditors, or other beneficiaries.

Your estate can include the home you own, other properties, cars, businesses, pets, and even simple things like jewelry, books, and collectibles. As mentioned earlier, anything that is of *value*.

To ensure your estate goes to people whom you care about and not to strangers, enter—estate planning. This refers to the process of arranging the management and distribution of one's estate during one's lifetime so that everything will be distributed according to one's wishes after their death.

To debate the importance of estate planning, here is a tale of a family. Mr. Barnes, an old widower, has five children and about twelve grandchildren. He has an estate that's worth $1,500,000. This includes several properties across the US, his vineyard business, home, a proud labrador, two cars, online brokerage accounts, bank accounts, and other personal belongings.

But he hasn't done any estate planning. He simply ignored writing a will or even thought of distributing his estate to his children and grandchildren. He eventually went on to die without a will. This led to a complicated court process, otherwise known as probate, where the state controls most of the estate disposal and it ended up with high legal fees and conflicts within the Barnes family for a piece of his estate.

As you can imagine, this may have turned out to be a very messy situation considering the wealth Barnes made and also looking at his family structure. If he had done his estate planning and assigned specific pieces of his estate to each beneficiary, all of these complications could have been reduced.

Because Barnes hasn't done his estate planning, there are a lot of unsettled affairs such as who's going to take over his vineyard business? How can they transfer their investment wealth to an online estate account? Who will take care of his beloved labrador?

But even if you do estate planning, it doesn't mean that you're out of the waters. Let's say Mr. Barnes did his estate planning but didn't update it regularly till his inevitable death. Just before his death, one of his children passed away and he was a beneficiary in taking over his vineyard business.

This can also lead to complications because Barnes failed to properly plan his contingent beneficiaries (basically a secondary beneficiary if the primary beneficiary doesn't inherit the estate) or update his estate plan. Thus, a well-crafted estate plan can ensure that your children inherit your assets without unnecessary legal hurdles.

Common Misconceptions

Unfortunately, many put off estate planning because there can be common misconceptions tied to it. I will bust some myths in this section.

The most common misconception I've seen is many think estate planning is for the wealthy. Let me tell you. It's crucial for anyone who wishes to control how their assets are handled after their death.

For instance, even a modest estate can benefit from a will to direct the distribution of personal belongings. Regardless of the size of your estate, it may be even $50,000, but it's all worth the value and to be preserved for future generations.

You wouldn't want even an estate of a small size to go through expensive probate cases and eventually have nothing left for your children after all of the money being used up from that estate itself (you read that right!).

Estates of small size without any will or estate plan have a higher risk of getting hit with a lot of damage compared to an estate of higher value. Therefore, every penny of your estate does count and is better off being used by your loved ones or people you care about.

Even if one does not have relatives alive or children, one's estate might end up going to the state if there was no estate plan behind it. Instead, it would've been better off going to charity, right? Hence, regardless of what one's wealth is, an estate plan is for *everyone*.

Another misconception is that having a will helps to avoid probate. Even though one might like to avoid a probate, this isn't true. Even if you have a will or not, a probate inevitably happens. The only difference is when you have a will, your family saves more time and money, has fewer conflicts, and has fewer complications when compared to going through a probate without a will.

Another misconception many think is that once you have made an estate plan, you're good to go. Even though this may be somewhat true, it isn't exactly the case. An estate plan prepares for the inevitable and it should be something that you should revisit often to update.

There can be major changes in your life such as the death of a spouse, or children, or the birth of a child or grandchild. Of course, there can be changes to your estate such as purchasing new investments or selling some of your assets. All of these can affect your current estate plan and it is suggested to review your estate plan every couple of years or whenever these major life changes occur.

The Need for Estate Planning

So, from what we have learned so far, regardless of estate size, planning is a necessity, especially for the following reasons:

- preserving your assets and belongings for future generations
- providing financial support for your spouse or children
- minimizing legal expenses and taxes
- enabling appointed individuals to execute decisions on your behalf in the event of you being incapacitated
- doing good deeds by giving away your assets for a noble cause or a charity
- have peace of mind and know that your wishes will be fulfilled after you move on

Estate planning is essential if you want to avoid intestacy, reduce estate taxes, and ensure that your wishes are followed. If you don't have an estate plan, your respective state laws can determine asset distribution, which might end up not aligning with your desires and it is a scenario that no one would want.

Key Components of Estate Planning

In this section, we will break down estate planning by knowing the essential components that make up a typical estate plan. They are as follows:

Wills and Trusts

The first component includes two things that can protect your assets (or estate) and facilitate the smooth distribution of them to rightful beneficiaries—wills and trusts.

Let's talk about wills. A will is essentially a legal document that articulately communicates who will receive your assets and properties after your death. In simple words, it is a document that enlists your wishes.

To ensure all of your wishes in your will are fulfilled as exactly as you listed, this is where you should name an executor. An executor's major role is to carry out all of the directions you have written in your will.

In your will, you can name intricate details such as even naming guardians for minors who would need a dependent. As a result, it helps to execute your asset distribution perfectly.

Now, let's understand what trusts are and how different they are from wills. A trust is typically a legal arrangement where you preserve your assets or estate to a trustee, who on your behalf, will protect them for your beneficiaries to receive them upon your death.

A trust can be of two kinds—revocable and irrevocable. Revocable trusts allow you to retain control over your assets which are placed in the trust during your lifetime and you would have the option to revoke or alter terms anytime.

On the other hand, irrevocable trusts, as the name suggests, mean that once you place your assets in the trust, they will no longer be yours, and it is ultimately preserved for the named beneficiaries. In a nutshell, you can't reverse the action when you place in such trusts.

The major benefit of irrevocable trusts and why they seem like a popular choice is that when assets get appreciated in the trust, they won't be subjected to estate taxes.

As you can see, trusts are different from wills as they can help you bypass probates because trusts remove legal complications and preserve specific assets for named beneficiaries. But remember it would be only for assets that you put in a trust that avoids probate. If there are assets that aren't in a trust, then it would without a doubt be exposed to probate. So, that's a very important point to keep in your mind always.

Powers of Attorney

The next component addresses having an individual or individuals who will make important decisions on your behalf. There will be a time whether you are seriously ill or after your death, to make some important decisions—whether it is general or financial.

The thing is you are either not there or do not have the mental capacity to make these decisions. This is why having a Power of Attorney can be crucial and thus, makes an integral part of your estate plan. They are like your agent who have the power to make important financial and other decisions on your behalf.

The implications of not appointing a Power of Attorney can be vividly experienced especially if you are single as the court will often select someone else to fulfill this role. In most families, this role is assigned to a spouse or a trustworthy family member.

Health Care Directives

The next component addresses your healthcare needs. This is where having a healthcare directive can assist you in times when you are unable to do anything and require specific healthcare needs to be fulfilled.

The health care directive consists of a living will and a health care proxy. I know what you might be thinking—there's also a will for when you're alive?! Though the name suggests that, it's a written will where you give directions for your healthcare needs if you fall terminally ill.

On the other hand, a healthcare proxy typically appoints a person who will make important medical decisions on your behalf when you are unable to do so.

If you are thinking about why this is an important component that needs to be added to your estate plan, then think of a situation where you do fall terminally ill, and this can be an emotional and stressful moment for your family members. They would be arguing over some healthcare decisions and having different opinions on how you should be taken care of. Therefore, having a health care directive can help carry out medical decisions as you wish and remove all the stress and burden from your family.

Beneficiary Designations

The final integral component addresses who will receive your estate. An estate plan won't be complete without naming the parties that will receive each portion of your assets or properties.

In this part, it should be kept updated regularly as your wishes can change depending on important life events and of course, in the end, it is your choice. Therefore, it has to be thoroughly reviewed and updated with care as it's the most important step to determine your estate getting into the hands of the right people.

Estate Planning and Your Family

Before wrapping up the chapter, you have to understand that estate planning is more of an emotional decision rather than doing it for the namesake. Estate planning is for your family, it is ensuring they move on from a time when it can be very emotional seeing you leave this world.

Even if you don't have a family, there are people in your life that you care about and support. It could be your friends, or someone you feel that needs and deserves your help.

You could be doing estate planning that aligns with your important values such as giving away your estate to support a charity or a cause you believe in. Everyone has different beliefs and important people with whom they have strengthened bonds within their lifetime.

Protecting Your Loved Ones

In a time when your family members are missing you after you have moved on, estate planning helps in providing for your loved ones in your absence.

Just like how life insurance can help, estate planning helps to provide assets and financial aid to your family when you are no longer around.

Even if your children or grandchildren are minors, with estate planning, you can name guardians in your will that will help protect your children's future and give you peace of mind.

Ensuring Financial Security

Estate planning helps to clearly outline how you are going to distribute your assets and also all the assets that are set up in trusts. As a result, it helps to preserve and guarantee financial security for your family. They can keep living in your absence.

Estate planning also helps protect your inheritance from creditors.

If you have debts, you can choose from which assets or bank accounts your creditors can take the money from and leave the most important assets for your family—thus, freeing them from any financial burden.

Preserving Family Harmony

Ultimately, anyone would want to see their family members in harmony and prevent disputes in the event of their death. By having a clear estate plan, you will remove any potential disputes such as misunderstandings, claims for each estate, and other sentimental conflicts.

The right actions one can take to create a robust estate plan are appointing the right professionals to work with to facilitate the process, drawing up a will and setting up a trust, thoroughly naming and reviewing your beneficiaries, and communicating the plan with your loved ones.

I know the last step might seem hard as it's easier said than done, but it is important to go through it and it will eventually preserve harmony within the family.

And that's for the fundamentals! You have got a brief overview of what estate planning is all about and how mega-important it can be for you and your family's future.

With the basics in hand, let's start with the first actionable step in your estate planning journey—assessing your situation.

Chapter 2:

Assessing Your Estate Planning Needs

Everyone's life is different.

Your estate plans shouldn't be like how your parents planned out, or how your friends are doing theirs.

It should be tailored to your situation because every individual's situation and needs are *unique*.

This chapter will help you understand how you can tailor your estate plan to meet your family's and financial goals' specific needs by learning a few basic guidelines.

Personal and Family Assessment

The first step you must take is to assess your personal and family situation. This is an integral step to identify your estate planning goals and identify wishes that matter to you.

The following should be addressed under this particular assessment:

Identifying Assets and Liabilities

I won't lie because this can be a dry and often challenging task but an internal part of your estate assessment. The first step is to evaluate your estate inventory. In other words, find out what your estate is worth.

This is simply done by including all of your assets, evaluating their worth, and subtracting all of the debt you currently have. The remainder will provide you with an accurate value of your estate that you can give to your family.

The last thing your family would need to find out is that despite knowing all of the assets you have, you need to pay off debts that you owe to creditors and they are usually the ones that will be paid first when the probate is ongoing and then your family gets the remainder of your estate (We will learn more about this in subsequent chapters).

Now, let us look at what I mean by your assets. Here are a few examples of assets that can be added to your estate inventory (*What Is Included in an Estate Inventory? - SmartAsset,* n.d.):

- Your home, real estate, and other properties.

- Your bank accounts—including checking, savings, money market accounts, and CDs.

- Your investment accounts—including brokerage, IRAs, margin accounts, HSAs, and college savings.

- Your business (can include all forms of legal structures).
- Intellectual property such as patents, copyrights, and trademarks.
- Stocks and bonds.
- Assets that you own outside your state and foreign countries.
- Your vehicles—including cars, vans, trucks, and motorcycles.
- Plans related to your workplace such as pension plans, 401(k)s, 403(b)s, etc.
- Insurance policies such as life insurance, long-term care, and disability insurance.
- Personal belongings such as your household items, collectibles, art, books, jewelry, etc.
- Debt due to you (this can also include unpaid wages, employee benefits, commission, etc.).

Once you have assessed and added all of your assets to your estate inventory, you get a clear picture of the status of these assets.

For example, is the property that you own in foreign jurisdictions worth something? Do you still have the papers organized that confirm you as the owner of the property? and so on.

Next, add the liabilities to your estate inventory. Here are a few examples of liabilities (*What Is Included in an Estate Inventory? - SmartAsset,* n.d.):

- your mortgage loans (associated with every property you own)
- outstanding loan payments (includes personal loans, business loans, student loans, vehicle loans, etc)
- credit card debt and open lines of credit
- unpaid utility bills
- liabilities from existing lawsuits
- outstanding medical bills
- taxes you owe
- any other outstanding debt
- account for debt related to your post-death costs such as funeral expenses, administrative fees, and legal fees

Having a catalog of your assets and liabilities is necessary not only to understand your net worth but also to have your executor access them during probate.

The executor is responsible for accounting everything in your estate inventory so that all of the administrative fees are paid, the debts are paid to creditors, and the beneficiaries get what was stated in your wishes.

Understanding Family Dynamics

After evaluating your estate inventory, you will need to understand your family dynamics.

Firstly, evaluate the number of children, grandchildren, and other family members you have and want to incorporate as beneficiaries in your wishes.

Then, consider understanding your relationships with each one of them. This helps you identify potential conflicts within your family that could affect your estate planning. Common examples include sibling rivalries or divorce.

There are circumstances if you are a remarried individual, you may need to balance inheritance between children from your first marriage and your new spouse. This will be touched upon in detail under the "special considerations" section.

Future Goals and Aspirations

Understanding your family dynamics and also your estate inventory helps you to define what you hope to achieve with your estate.

This can depend on the individual, but a common example is ensuring your children's or grandchildren's education needs are met or supporting a spouse when your time is up.

This is an important part of the planning process because when you define your goals and aspirations, it helps you to make your estate planning much easier and with less confusion.

You do not want to be in a position where you are deciding who is going to inherit your home for example and have your children fight over it. When you have established goals after evaluating your family dynamics, you will know who to give your home to.

For instance, you could give it to one of your children who has fewer financial resources and needs to raise their children, compared to your other children who are more successful. You would even have reasons to justify your wishes and make it transparent to your family.

Special Considerations

Despite evaluating your estate inventory and your family dynamics, there can be special situations where you need to pay extra attention.

This includes implementing special strategies to solve complex situations.

Here are three special situations that you need to do more thinking with your estate plan:

Blended Families

There are situations where your estate planning might need a bit more pondering if you have a blended family. This means you have remarried and also have to consider children from your previous marriage and current marriage.

Despite blended families being labeled as a "special" consideration, it isn't much different from how one evaluates an average family dynamics when making their estate plan.

The only common mistake you need to avoid is failing to update your will regularly—especially after a divorce or getting remarried.

Taking a real-life example, if you have remarried to a new spouse but have the will you made from your previous marriage and children, it will create complications.

In estate planning, updating your will regularly after *every* life-changing event is a must. This includes divorces, marriages, birth of a child, etc. Therefore, it should be a natural mechanism to revisit your estate plan after you get a divorce after you remarry, and after the birth of your child in the new marriage.

There are estate planning options that are specially catered to blended families. Here are a few:

- A **marital bypass trust** allows your assets to be passed to the surviving spouse, and also at the same time, designate residual assets for children after the spouse's death.

- **Family trusts** can help foresee assets heading into a combined trust after the death of the first spouse. This structure allows the surviving parent to decide how they will designate assets to each child's needs.

- Without using trusts, you can designate assets to each child in both marriages. This can be stated in your will. Whichever heir you don't mention as a beneficiary in your will, will not inherit any of your estate. This is a straightforward option but can be best discussed with your spouse and children to avoid potential conflicts.

For special situations such as estate planning for blended families, this requires you to put more thought and also hire a lawyer to assist you as special circumstances can require professional solutions.

Business Ownership

If you have a business, it would always be in your best interest to plan for a successor to carry on your venture. However, here are a few considerations and options you may want to account as a business owner who is doing an estate plan:

- **Use your will:** When you state in your will who will take over your business, it can be clear. Moreover, you would want to appoint your power of attorney and healthcare directive to make business decisions on your behalf when you are unable to do so.

- **Family-owned businesses:** One common mistake one can make is not understanding the implications of transferring a family-owned business. For instance, if you pass it to your children, this means their future spouse will jointly own business assets. Likewise, when you pass it to your spouse, this means their future spouse can jointly own it. It requires careful thinking and sorting out issues within the family.

- **Buy-sell agreement:** For businesses with multiple owners, a buy-sell agreement defines who can buy out an owner's share. The benefit of this agreement helps keep the business at the helm of existing owners despite the death of one of the owners.

- **Life and Disability insurance:** Having life insurance coverage helps to provide for your family after you pass away. On top of that, you can name the business as a beneficiary so that it provides an income source for the business to keep its operations running in your absence. Likewise, disability insurance works similarly if you become disabled and can no longer contribute to your business.

- **Succession plan:** A succession plan is a document that outlines how you, your company, and your family will transition into ownership. This is a more formal document that analyzes the business structure, opportunities, etc. but is closely linked to your wishes that you state in your will.

Sometimes, it can be simple to discuss with relevant parties to understand their interests. For example, you wouldn't want to give away your business to a child if they are not interested or responsible for managing something big.

There can be other family members or other connections that express their interest better and are a better fit to be the successor to your business. Therefore, ownership of a business is something serious and should be considered carefully.

Charitable Intentions

The last consideration you will need to pay close attention to is when you intend to leave a portion of your estate to charity.

When it comes to tax implications, donations basically reduce estate taxes and since they are "gifts", this means they are exempt from inheritance tax.

There are a few ways in which you can have your estate plan to include your charitable intentions. Instructions that you leave within your estate plan or will to allocate portions of your assets to charitable organizations are typically known as charitable bequests.

You can even name charities as named beneficiaries in certain accounts such as your life insurance policies or retirement accounts. In addition, a charitable gift annuity is a contract where a charity provides you, as the donor, a fixed monthly or quarterly payout in exchange for the gift they received from you. This usually is agreed till the end of your life, where eventually the remainder of the gift will be transferred to the charity after your death.

Some trusts can also help you ease the process of providing charitable donations as part of your estate plan. One trust in particular is the charitable remainder trust. This particular type of trust helps to keep providing income to charitable beneficiaries during your lifetime and transfer the remainder to the organization after your death.

Setting Clear Objectives

As the final segment of this chapter, we will put more emphasis on your estate planning objectives and the legacy you want to leave behind.

Short-Term and Long-Term Goals

The most efficient way of setting and pursuing goals is to categorize them into short-term and long-term goals. This provides you with more clarity when crafting your estate plan.

Short-term goals are immediate objectives that can be fulfilled within a shorter timeframe. This can include appointing guardians for your minor children or drafting a will.

On the other hand, long-term goals are looking at the big picture, that can take a little longer to set up and achieve. This can include preserving your wealth across generations or setting up an educational trust.

However, these goals can be vague and can hinder your estate planning process. This is why you should try making your long-term and short-term goals definitive, realistic, and measurable till you achieve them.

I will give you a few examples that can help inspire some estate planning goals of your own:

- My estate planning goal is to make sure my family avoids the pain of going through probate. To avoid probate, I already know I can preserve my assets with trusts, name beneficiaries for complex assets, establish jointly-owned accounts, or even gift those assets to my loved ones before I die. All of these can help bypass probate.

- One of my estate planning goals is to protect my home taken away by creditors. This helps me to address my mortgage situation so that my home doesn't be at risk of foreclosure when after I die. Moreover, to pay off other debts, I can name in my will or estate plan assets that the executor should use to pay creditors, and this would mean that my home is safe.

- My goal is to make sure all of the inherited assets stay within the family. This is because I could be worried in situations where my spouse remarries and has the assets passed to her spouse if she dies. In this case, I could look to have these assets owned by trusts which help to stay within the family as I intended.

You can see I went into a little more detail and this helps to brainstorm options and create an estate plan that accomplishes all of your intended wishes.

Protecting Vulnerable Family Members

There are situations where your estate plan needs to cater to family members that require extra care. This may be because they are disabled or are unable to care for themselves. This should be part of your consideration.

For example, you can utilize a special needs trust for a disabled child. This makes sure they are provided for without any skepticism regarding their eligibility for government benefits.

Leaving a Lasting Legacy

Last but not least, determine how you want to be remembered. What values and contributions you would want to leave behind that define your legacy?

This can depend on you. Maybe you would want to fund a scholarship in your name which helps to support future generations of students in a particular field of interest.

Or it can be creating a school in your hometown so that you become an example of where you were born and brought up or you desire to help your people.

This can be very personal to you and only you will know that when you are doing your estate planning. All of these tasks, whether it is evaluating your estate inventory, understanding your family better, or understanding your deepest desires and wishes, it helps to remove friction and provide a clear mindset to create a well-thought estate plan.

Now that you have addressed knowing your needs, let's delve into creating a comprehensive will.

Chapter 3:

Crafting Your Will

Dying *without* a will leads to more severe consequences for your family than it does if you pass away *with* a will.

You are probably eager to learn how so.

We have learned the fundamentals of estate planning and how you can start the entire process by evaluating your needs first. Now, let's move on to learning in-depth about wills.

Understand that wills are a *part* of your estate planning and shouldn't be something that you consider as a separate entity.

This chapter will help you uncover the critical importance of a will in directing your legacy and also a few insights on avoiding common pitfalls that can undermine your genuine intentions.

The Importance of a Will

Legal Necessities

As I mentioned briefly in Chapter 1, a will is a legal document communicating your wishes. But there is something more to why an average American has to have a will when they pass away and know the consequences of not having one.

Let's understand it by recalling the tale of Mr. Barnes. If you remember one particular detail: Mr. Barnes died without having written a will.

According to the court, he is said to have passed away "intestate." In other words, he died without having a Will. This meant the state could now apply *its* laws and administer his estate.

This turned out to be a horrible experience for his family during the probate court process. Creditors were able to have their hands on many of Mr. Barnes' precious assets since he owed a lot of debt and some of those assets should've been kept for his children and grandchildren—including their home, land, vehicles, and so on.

Now, what if Mr. Barnes had a will? First and foremost, a will doesn't avoid the probate court process. His family still has to go through that lengthy process, but they wouldn't be facing such a horrible situation as I mentioned earlier.

If Mr. Barnes died with a will, he would have been said to have passed away "testate." This is because whoever makes a will is known as a "testator" (keep that in mind). In his will, he would have clearly outlined the assets he intends to give to his family members and also specified the assets that his creditors can access to settle his debts.

Do you see the contrast here?

Controlling Asset Distribution

A will's major function is to specify how you are going to distribute your assets to beneficiaries.

Take, for example, your home, business, land, real estate properties, bank accounts, and so on. You have the right to outline how you intend to distribute them and this depends on you.

You could give your home to your surviving spouse, your son to take over your business, and your daughter to inherit one of your other properties. Moreover, you can specify that your creditors can use one of your less-worth properties as a means to settle your debts with creditors.

Besides pinpointing who gets your assets, you may be required to share detailed instructions for the beneficiaries on how you can access some accounts—especially digital accounts.

For instance, you may have loads of digital assets such as online bank accounts, brokerage accounts, social media accounts, and even digital files stored on your computer. All of these will require passwords to access them.

These details are better off mentioned separately from your will in a document called "letter of instruction." In this document, you write more personal wishes such as how you want your funeral done and how to access your digital accounts.

Minimizing Family Conflicts

A will helps in minimizing potential family conflicts. Without a will, there will be ambiguity surrounding who gets your assets, and especially when the state gets its hands on the estate, no one in your family is going to be happy with that.

With a will, you can leave specific assets to each family member with a reason for your intentions on leaving that particular asset for them.

You end up reducing potential conflicts among family members after you pass away.

Writing Your Will

Now that you have understood the importance of having a will, I will walk through how you should craft one.

Before writing your will, remind yourself of your estate planning goals, have your inventory checklist with you, and as a result, you can start organizing how you want your assets distributed and your debt paid off.

Writing a will is somewhat of a formal process. To create a valid will, you must meet the following requirements:

Legal age- This is a no-brainer. You need to be at least the legal age of majority (18 years in most states in the U.S.) to create a valid will.

- **Testamentary capacity:** In simple words, this means you have to be of sound mind and be aware that you are creating a will and also willingly accept that you are creating one. This is typically related to meeting the essentials of making any contract valid.

- **Handwritten or typed:** Your will has to be handwritten or typed in words to make it valid. In very few states, you will have them recognize oral wills or holographic wills.

- **Signed and witnessed:** Apart from including other minor details such as date, you need to sign your will—and wait for it—have at least two witnesses or more see you sign it. This can depend on the state you are based in, but most states require at least a couple of witnesses in a mini-formal ceremony where they witness you officially signing your will. In some states, they may even ask you to notarize your will.

So, the above conditions help you to make a will valid under the law. Let's find out what the contents of your will should be.

Choosing an Executor

An executor (sometimes referred to as a personal representative) is an individual you appoint to carry out the instructions you stated in your will.

In other words, this is the person who is going to make your wishes a reality and also be heavily involved during the probate process—by accessing your estate, managing it, notifying creditors and beneficiaries, filing and paying legal fees, doing all the estate accounting, and finally distributing your assets.

As you can see, the executor has a major role to play after your death. Executors usually get paid for their services. Especially if you choose one of your close family members to be an executor, you might want to understand their potential to fulfill such a role.

Especially if you have a pool of potential candidates to be your executor, you should measure them by the following traits:

- trustworthiness

- availability

- social competency

- financial knowledge

- patience

- organized

If the individual checks all of the above traits with flying colors, then they may be the right fit to be your executor. It is also important to be aware that you can hire multiple executors if required. This is done in cases where someone's estate is big and complex.

One can even hire an institution to be an executor, but in most cases, people either appoint one of their immediate family members or a professional (like an attorney) to be the executor of their will.

The consequences of not naming an executor mean that a court appoints an individual of their choice to manage your estate settlement—which might not suit your family's best interests. This court-appointed individual is referred to as an "administrator." When a person dies without a will or "intestate," the court ends up appointing an administrator to manage the estate.

This is why naming your executor in your will is mega-important because an executor has the fiduciary duty to act in the best interest of your beneficiaries. If an executor fails to do so and commits a minor mistake or in some cases fraud, the beneficiaries have every right to spot these mistakes and request for another executor. Hence, take time to choose your ideal executor.

Detailing Asset Distribution

The next important part of your will's content should include how you want your assets to be distributed. In other words, specify to whom particular assets should be distributed and how. This can include specific gifts as well to avoid ambiguity.

I will provide an example of how you can specifically outline each asset distribution.

Let's say you have a real estate property that is worth a lot. Instead of giving it entirely to one child, you can bequeath a specific piece of that real estate to one child, and allocate equivalent value in stocks to another child.

Do you see how you can detail your asset distribution in the way that you intend to?

You even have the control to set some portion of your estate or assets to be given to your favorite local charity or to support a cause. Thus, you also fulfill philanthropic intentions that make you remembered for your kind actions after you pass away.

While specifying how you want your assets distributed, you should name your beneficiaries. It is easy to execute this part especially if you have everything planned out, but it is also important to name a "contingent" beneficiary.

Contingent beneficiaries act as backup beneficiaries because imagine this situation: You decided to give away your home to your son, but what if he decides to turn down the inheritance? What if he can't be contacted or may be presumed dead?

In such cases, you can name for instance your daughter to be the contingent beneficiary so that she inherits the home if your son doesn't. It is important to include them so that the state doesn't get to decide who gets a specific asset if the primary beneficiary doesn't inherit it.

Providing for Minors and Dependents

While writing a will, designating your beneficiaries is one important aspect, but caring for minors and dependents should be your top priority.

You may be quite young when you are writing a will and might have children who are minors. If you are older, you may have grandchildren who are minors. Nevertheless, minor children need someone to take care of them after their parents' death.

This is where the purpose of appointing a guardian comes to your aid. A guardian is someone who will take care of your minors or dependents when you are unable to or pass away.

Guardians are also needed when you distribute certain properties or assets to minor children. For example, if you decide that your minor son or grandson to inherit one of your properties, then this means they won't inherit them till they turn 18.

Your guardians will have custody of the property and then give it to your son or grandson after they turn 18. This is the same case when you entrust guardians with bank accounts or digital assets till minors reach the legal age to have them *legally* owned by them.

When you are appointing a guardian for a minor, remember to choose those who are willing to do it and hold such responsibility. In many cases, it is easy to pick a guardian. For instance, you choose your son and daughter-in-law to be guardians of your grandchild.

However, in situations, where one needs to handle complex assets and the minor is heavily dependent on you, you should take your time to choose the right guardian for them.

Not only do minors require a guardian, but any dependents in your family who require special attention. Additionally, pets are also family, especially if you have one. Hence, you can even appoint someone to take care of your pet after you pass away.

Just like we mentioned about contingent beneficiaries a while back, it can be important to include backup guardians if the primary guardian either passes away or is unable to look after your minor children.

You can even have trusts established within your will so it can help manage assets for minors and dependents, but you will learn more about trusts in the next chapter.

After creating your will, and having it signed and witnessed, you have officially drafted a comprehensive will. You choose to store it safely in a safe or entrust it with your attorney. It can be important to have copies of your original will because, in the next section, we will go through some common mistakes you need to avoid.

Common Pitfalls to Avoid

There can be minor or major errors that can lead to confusion regarding your wills and sometimes, even the validity of one.

I will walk you through an incident that could happen when one of the family members or beneficiaries questions some of the decisions you made in your will.

This can mainly happen maybe because they are not happy, or sense something isn't right. To challenge your will means to "contest a will."

Contesting a will is a costly legal process and beneficiaries wouldn't necessarily do that until they can prove one of the following:

- Your original will doesn't exist or was destroyed by you.

- You had a lack of testamentary capacity when making the will—meaning you were not of sound mind when you made it.

- You were under the influence of someone when making the will.

- Your will wasn't signed properly, or the witnesses can't confirm seeing you sign it.

These are things you don't need to worry about especially if you have drafted a well-comprehensible and valid will that meets the essential legal requirements.

To address factors such as "claiming" the original will get destroyed by you or misplaced, you can always entrust your original will to your attorney or a close family member and also have copies with a few family members to show that your will is valid and wasn't destroyed by you.

When a will contest happens, the court confirms if the will was misplaced or destroyed by you—just to understand if it ever existed. Courts account for misplaced wills as valid as long as the copies (of the will) show their existence.

If the person contesting the will loses, they end up paying lengthy fees regardless. So, in most cases, contests aren't worth it especially if the estate value or inheritance they are fighting for exceeds the legal costs and their time.

From your side, you can do the following to avoid any common errors that most testators do:

Vague Language

The worst thing one can do when writing a will is to make instructions unclear and pretty vague.

Consider the following two sentences and decide which sounds clearer to you if you were an executor reading a will:

- "I leave all of my assets to my child."

- "I leave all of my assets including the family home situated in Minnesota, a real estate property in Florida, a property situated in Texas, and my investment brokerage account to my son, Brian Howson."

Pretty sure you chose the second one.

The first one was pretty vague and could potentially lead to a lot of unanswered questions. Whereas, the second one was clear, specific, and removes ambiguity.

The above one was just an example but as someone writing a will, you should ensure everything is clear and specific so that your executor will thoroughly carry out your wishes just like you want.

Not Updating Regularly

Another common mistake one can make is to write the will and completely forget about it. Not regularly reviewing a will and updating it can lead to several consequences.

Let's say a man drafted his will when he was 35. He decided to leave his entire estate to his wife. But fast-forward a few years later his life situation changes. His wife and he are divorced and he dies at the age of 50.

Because he didn't update his will, his entire estate would end up going to his ex-wife (which he wouldn't have intended to do just before he died) instead of let's say, his kids or spouse from his second marriage.

This is because his *last* will or testament counts! You can regularly update your will and have the most recent one the "last" will that will decide the fate of your estate.

The above example is just one of many. After you make a will, many things can happen. A beneficiary could die and this would lead to questions about where the money or asset should go, and there could be other changes in your life situation that require you to update your will.

You may have two questions: So, *how* do we update it, and *when*?

You can update your will by making use of one of the two options:

- **Codicil:** This is like an additional document attached to your will. You can state all the modifications in it. This is recommended if you want to make *minor* adjustments.

- **Create a new will:** This is recommended when you are making major changes or too many changes. You can draft a new will all over again, repeat the legal requirements and proceedings, and then revoke all of your previous wills.

When it comes to knowing *when* to update your will, always account for major life changes. This includes marriage, divorce, birth of a child, adoption of a child, death of a beneficiary, acquiring or selling assets, starting or closing a business, etc.

Whenever any significant event happens, your first thought should be to revisit your will, re-check the beneficiaries, and update them regularly. Yes, it may seem like a tedious process but it is vital!

Overlooking Digital Assets

Another common mistake one can make is to overlook their digital assets which include digital files, documents, spreadsheets, websites, online accounts, digital currencies, and so on. In a will, you will need to decide who inherits them.

I have already mentioned that you can include a letter of instruction to specify how you can access certain digital assets.

Besides digital assets, many can overlook the residuary estate. This refers to the remainder of your estate after all the debts and legal fees have been paid and all distributions have been made.

Not everything you may account for in your inventory list has to be perfect. There can be situations where your property is worth a lot more than you estimated or there could be unpaid income you weren't aware of.

This is why you should include a residuary clause in your will and name someone (probably a close family member) to inherit the residuary estate so it doesn't simply go to the state.

Wills are crucial to state your wishes and best intentions. You have learned the importance of it and how to have it drafted and made legally valid. However, wills are only the first integral component of your estate plan.

The next chapter will discuss more about trusts—a medium for preserving assets from creditors and *avoiding* probate. Curious to learn more?

Chapter 4:

Understanding and Utilizing Trusts

"My neighbor didn't need to go through probate!"

As soon as one of my close friends spoke these words, I dropped my fork on the dinner table with a sign of disbelief and astonishment.

This was the first time I heard someone making such a statement. All those years I thought, despite having a will, a family still needed to go through the daunting court procedure to get their estate settled.

But how wrong I was! I felt I was kept in the dark. I was mesmerized to learn more.

My friend went on to continue the intriguing tale. After his neighbor's mother passed away at the age of 76, they had their estate settled in private and within less than six months.

Their kids and grandkids got their inheritance and didn't even see the courtroom. That's when I learned that their mother preserved all of the assets in a "trust".

This was initially set up by their father who passed away earlier, but their mother was able to access the trust's inheritance during her lifetime for medical needs and after her death, all of the assets have been distributed to the heirs.

Establishing trust is another vital part of your estate plan. One should not ignore this.

This chapter will help you understand what it is, the various types of trusts available, and how they offer asset protection and flexibility in your estate management.

Types of Trusts

First and foremost, let's understand what a trust means. By legal definition, a trust is a legal arrangement where a trustee holds rights to hold and manage the assets of a trustor to benefit the beneficiaries.

In a trust, there are three major parties involved:

1. You have the "trustor," the one who makes the trust and transfers his assets to them. In this case, it would be you looking to preserve your assets for your beneficiaries. A trustor can also be referred to as a grantor, settlor, or trustmaker.

2. The "trustee" manages the trust and holds the assets for you. The trustee has to follow the trust's terms and provisions and act in the best interests of distributing to the beneficiaries.

3. Then, you have the "beneficiary," that is someone who will receive the inheritance, funds, or assets after the trustor passes away.

From this, you already have a good idea of how a trust works. You set up a trust, transfer your estate's assets into the trust, and after your death, the trustee will distribute them to the beneficiaries.

Trusts come in various types. As various individuals have different goals and family dynamics, having trust for different purposes is a blessing.

I will walk you through the major types of trusts that you should know about:

Revocable vs. Irrevocable Trusts

As a trustor, knowing the difference between a revocable and irrevocable trust is crucial.

A revocable trust is a type of trust where you, as the trustor, can change the terms and provisions of the trust for any reason and at any time—including revoking it.

On the other hand, an irrevocable trust is a type of trust where once you create it, you cannot change it, and nor can you revoke it. In other words, you simply can't reverse the action.

So, for example, if you set up an irrevocable trust and transfer all of your assets—including your home, other real estate properties, land, vehicles, bank accounts, etc.—this means you no longer own these assets.

It will be under the name of the trust, and you cannot reverse this action. Eventually, after your death, these assets will be distributed to the intended beneficiaries.

Now you must be thinking that irrevocable trusts might sound like a bad idea. But it will surprise you that many end up setting irrevocable trusts. Why so? Irrevocable trusts help for three major reasons:

- It helps minimize estate tax because the trustor transfers ownership of his assets to the trust, thus, reducing his taxable estate.

- It helps protect your assets away from creditors because these assets are no longer owned by you and are kept for your beneficiaries.

- Most trusts that cater to providing for minors or those that may have special needs are irrevocable. This provides you with more options.

Understanding the benefits of both revocable and irrevocable trusts can help you provide flexibility in your estate management.

For instance, if you have a pretty large estate, and want to minimize your taxable estate or even avoid probate, you can transfer your assets into an irrevocable trust.

You may even have a situation where you have some assets that you want to get access to during your lifetime, then this helps you to put those assets into a revocable trust—so that you get access to it and revoke it anytime you want.

Assets that you are 100% certain that you want to preserve for your beneficiaries can be transferred to an irrevocable trust.

Special Needs Trusts

There are situations in your family where you may need to pay special attention to someone who is physically or mentally disabled and may need lifetime care.

Special needs trusts are created for that purpose. It is catered to individuals (under the age of 65) who face physical or mental disability and who will require financial support after the trustor passes away.

This financial support also includes being eligible for government aid such as SSI or Medicaid.

There are three types of special needs trusts:

- **First-party:** This trust is funded using the beneficiary's assets and is filed by the parent, grandparent, or any other family member.

- **Third-party:** The trustor funds it with their assets to benefit the disabled beneficiary to access and have control over the trust.

- **Pooled:** In this trust, a non-profit holds the money and distributes it.

Living Trusts

A living trust is typically another name for a revocable trust—but its main idea is that it is established by you during your lifetime.

The benefit of having a living trust is that you have control over the assets within the trust, and this makes sure your beneficiaries benefit from it after you pass away.

However, as it is a revocable trust, this leads to a particular challenge. It is not an ideal "asset protection" hub when compared to irrevocable trusts, so your creditors can still get their hands on your assets during your lifetime and when you pass away.

Since living trusts are established during your lifetime, that means there is a particular trust that is established after you die. This trust is known as a testamentary trust.

This is a type of trust that you include in your will to have it take effect once you pass away. However, having a testamentary trust doesn't avoid going through probate.

Other Types of Trusts

There are other specific types of trusts that you can take advantage of to cater to specific needs. I will briefly mention a few:

- **Credit Shelter Trusts:** Helps to lower estate tax and benefit heirs. Also known as family or bypass trusts.

- **Spendthrift Trusts:** Allows you to distribute your assets to beneficiaries over time, rather than all at once.

- **Asset Protection Trusts:** Primarily helps to protect assets from creditors. Asset protection trusts can be set up locally or even offshore.

- **Irrevocable Life Insurance Trusts:** Helps to immediately fund beneficiaries and removes its value from taxable estate.

- **Joint Trusts:** Spouses can make use of it to jointly distribute their assets to beneficiaries.

- **A-B Trusts:** Spouses can separate their assets into two trusts—A and B trusts to minimize taxation.

- **Charitable Trusts:** Set up to benefit a charitable organization. Includes two types—Charitable Lead Trusts (CLTs) and Charitable Remainder Trusts (CRTs).

- **Qualified Terminable Interest Property (QTIP) Trusts:** Helps provide for the surviving spouse and assets get distributed to beneficiaries after the surviving spouse's death.

- **Blind Trusts:** These trusts don't provide prior information on assets to beneficiaries, to minimize potential conflicts.

- **Trust Decanting:** This is the process of moving assets from an existing trust into a new trust with favorable terms and conditions.

This is the beauty of trust because it has many options that can be tailored to each individual's needs.

Keep reading to learn how you can set up a typical trust.

Setting Up a Trust

You can set up a trust by yourself, but it is usually better to have professional help such as having your attorney for guidance.

When setting up a trust, you have to first decide what type of trust you need.

This can be realized by reflecting on your estate planning goals and defining the purpose. I will provide a few considerations you need to have:

Is my goal to make sure my family avoids probate?

Is my goal to ensure my assets won't be touched by my creditors?

Is my goal to cater to dependents who require special needs?

Is my goal to provide ongoing financial support for my spouse?

This can give you an idea of what your ultimate goal is and choose a specific trust that helps you achieve them. This also helps you decide whether you require a trust that is revocable or irrevocable to cater to your needs.

After you have determined your ideal trust, follow these steps:

Choosing a Trustee

The next step is to pick the person who is going to manage your trust. A trustee would be the owner of the assets you put into the trust so you should spend some time choosing the right person.

A trustee can be a professional outside your family, but most usually choose a close family member as the trustee.

When picking a trustee, ensure the person has sufficient knowledge to manage funds/assets, file for taxes, and ensure they distribute the inheritance to beneficiaries.

A trustee cannot access money in the trust for their personal use. A trustee can also be a beneficiary, but they will only get their inheritance after your death or what the trust terms say.

You can also choose to remove a trustee if you find they aren't fulfilling the role as per your expectations. But this requires getting agreement from all beneficiaries that they agree with the change.

One minor error trustors make when appointing a trustee is failing to pick a successor trustee. If the primary trustee passes away or resigns from their duties, your successor trustee would be in charge of the trust then.

Having successor trustees allows you, the trustor, to even be a trustee of the trust. This is possible during your lifetime. After you pass away, your successor trustee will be in charge of the trust and will ensure the assets get distributed to beneficiaries.

Trust Conditions and Clauses

After picking your trustee and successor trustee, you need to create a trust document. You can either do this by yourself or have your attorney help you draft it.

In the trust document, you will list the trust's conditions, provisions, and clauses. An example of such provisions includes instructions on how you want assets distributed to your beneficiaries and when.

I will give you a couple of examples for clarity. Suppose one of your grandchildren is a minor. You want to give him one of your brokerage accounts so that he can use it to earn passive income through stock investing.

In normal circumstances, your grandson would have got his hands on your brokerage account as soon as he turned 18. However, you feel 18 is too young for him to manage a brokerage account. He could end up spending all the money casually and make poor investing decisions.

You feel by the age of 24, after he gets a college degree and becomes more financially responsible, he will manage the brokerage account better. Hence, you can state that your grandson should receive such an account after he turns 24.

Another example can resonate if you have a blended family. You can establish provisions that allow the surviving spouse of your new marriage to get access to the trust's funds so that your ex-spouse cannot access them.

You can insert terms and provisions for each of the assets you plan to distribute to beneficiaries. Once you name all the beneficiaries and the effective date on which the trust works, your trust document is ready.

According to your respective state laws, you may be required to have the trust document signed and notarized with witnesses.

Then, you have officially opened a trust or trust account. You can name the trust as it is crucial to distinguish it if you establish many trusts. For example, you can add your family name, along with the date of the trust's establishment for simplicity.

Funding the Trust

After opening your trust, that's when you can start transferring assets into your trust. This is known as "funding the trust."

Before learning how you can fund the trust, you may be wondering what assets can you transfer into a trust.

You can transfer any small-to-large assets that belong in your estate including:

- Your family home
- Real estate properties
- Business interests
- Retirement accounts such as IRA, 401(k)s
- Cash accounts such as savings accounts, checking accounts, money market accounts, and CDs
- Stocks or bonds
- Vehicles
- Collectibles, jewelry, art, antiques, etc.
- Intangible assets such as intellectual property
- Other personal belongings or assets

It is amazing to see how trusts can allow you to preserve your valuable assets and have them kept for your loved ones.

Transferring assets into a trust can be done through various options depending on the type of asset. These options include:

- You can title or retitle certain assets to the name of the trust or even designate the trust as the beneficiary.

- Close and reopen bank accounts under the trust's name.

- Change the beneficiary of certain insurance policies to the trust's name.

- For properties, utilize deed agreements to transfer ownership to the name of the trust.

- For smaller assets such as personal belongings and also intellectual property, create an "Assignment of Property Interest" to complete the transfer into your trust.

- You can create an "Assignment of Rights" if you own oil or mineral rights and want to transfer them into your trust.

Specific assets may require specific ways to move them into your trust. Hence, it is best to consult with your attorney to understand the risks of transferring and whether there are tax implications behind transferring such assets such as "transfer tax."

One thing that can be ignored is assets that are not accounted for or assets that you don't want to transfer into a trust until your death. For example, your car because you have an auto insurance tied to it.

In such situations, you can utilize a "Pour-over-will" where you can instruct to transfer certain assets into your trust after your death.

Benefits of Trusts

You have learned the various types of trusts and also how to set up one. Yet, many ignore making a trust because they find it too intimidating to establish one when compared to drafting a simple will.

But you must not make the same mistake and ignore establishing a Trust for your benefit and your family's.

To understand the importance of having a trust in your estate plan, here are the major benefits it offers:

Avoiding Probate

The biggest benefit of them all is trusts help to "bypass" the probate process. What do you mean by this?

Some assets can entirely avoid probate if you make use of the following:

- Have the asset co-owned with someone else.

- Have a "named" beneficiary on certain assets such as an insurance policy.

- Create a trust and transfer the assets into them.

As you can see, trusts allow you to preserve assets, but if you place all of your assets into a trust, your family will avoid the entire probate court procedure just like how my friend's neighbors did.

Going through probate is a long, costly, draining, and often painful experience for your family—especially after the emotional struggle they have to deal with your passing.

In such circumstances, probate ain't worth the hassle. Your family can end up saving time and money from such a legal process by having trusts.

Trusts can help avoid this and help distribute assets to your loved ones quickly. Living trusts are excellent when it comes to quickly transferring assets to your beneficiaries upon your death. It removes any uncertainty about whether your loved ones will receive their assets or not.

Tax Advantages

Trusts can benefit your tax planning in a good way. For most irrevocable trusts, it excludes the trust's assets from your taxable estate. As a result, you reduce estate taxes.

One example is considering an irrevocable trust that contains a life insurance policy. The added benefit to this move is that not only do your beneficiaries receive the compensation but they receive it tax-free.

There can be some assets transferred into a trust that appreciates in value and as a result, you could be subjected to capital gain taxes. But some trusts can help you transfer assets and not account for their appreciation, thus, reducing income tax.

Long-Term Asset Management

Trusts are a way to preserve assets and manage them over time. Asset protection is a necessity when you want to protect them from your creditors, beneficiaries' creditors, divorce settlements, and also from making poor financial decisions.

It is also a way to make distributions based on provisions and terms that are catered to the beneficiary's needs and circumstances.

You don't risk giving away all of the assets right after you die and can preserve some of them for the long term till you feel the time is right for some beneficiaries to inherit them.

You may realize that setting up a trust seems more important than writing a will so that pops up the question: should I set up my trust and ignore writing a will?

No, you shouldn't! Though trusts help to avoid probate, preserve assets, and reduce taxes, it doesn't account for assets that you didn't account for and could potentially be part of your estate.

If you died without a will, these assets could be decided by the state. Therefore, it is necessary to have BOTH a will and trust in your estate plan.

In the following chapters, we will learn more about the people you need to appoint who will be a crucial part of your estate plan, especially during unforeseeable circumstances like your healthcare needs.

Chapter 5:

Advanced Health Care Directives

"I don't think my father needs to be put on ventilation!"

These were words spoken by one of Mr. Collins' sons as the old man was in a permanent vegetative state and potentially nearing the end of his life.

Mr. Collins raised three bright and successful children—two sons and a daughter to be precise.

Having written his last will and set up a trust to benefit his children, one day he was rushed to the hospital after unexpectedly suffering from a cardiac arrest.

His three children rushed to the hospital, and they spent the whole day arguing with the doctor. It was a catastrophe as Mr. Collins was not receiving the medical attention he needed, and his children had different viewpoints.

One of his sons was adamant that his father received whatever the doctor suggested, and they all equally paid the bills.

The other son was reluctant to believe anything the doctor said, as he didn't believe in the "system" itself. In other words, he didn't want to be involved in paying hefty medical bills.

Meanwhile, the daughter was emotionally staring at her father's unconscious eyes, not knowing what to do.

The doctor even hit the nerve of one of the sons when he asked if Mr. Collins could donate one of his organs—during such an emotional time when his children were indecisive about what to do.

It was a sad and devastating situation that no family wants to experience. Unfortunately, it all happened due to Mr. Collins not having an appropriate health agent or a living will that stated the type of medical attention *he wished* to have!

This chapter will help you prepare for the unexpected by understanding and creating healthcare directives that honor your medical wishes.

Understanding Health Care Directives

The recent pandemic has taught us that life can change pretty fast, and we need to prepare for such unpredictable circumstances. One of the greatest assets to one is their health.

When you are terminally ill or in a condition where you are no longer in sound mind to make decisions or act, this is where having someone to address your medical needs can be crucial.

Health care directives or advance directives are essentially legal documents that outline instructions on what medical care *you* require and they will take effect according to your wishes.

Having a health care directive not only would've saved Mr. Collin's imminent death but also prevented his children from worrying too much about making decisions in such a tense and emotional time.

In other words, they would have had peace of mind knowing that their father wanted the exact medical care he asked for and also had someone he trusted to make decisions on his behalf.

Living Wills

The first thing you need to include in your health care directive is a living will. Yes, a will is originally for fulfilling your wishes after your death, but there is also a will for fulfilling your wishes when you're alive—your medical needs in particular.

In your living will, you can outline the list of medical treatments you consent to and would want to keep you alive and also address other intentions such as donating an organ.

Just like a regular will, you will need to have your living will or forms to be signed or notarized and have them witnessed. Moreover, you will be required to review them every few years and update them just like you would for your regular will.

Though a regular will may require more updating due to major life events, a living will may also require the same. As time goes on, your medical needs may differ and this may call for an important and immediate update in your living will.

Also, if there are major life events that are not medically related, such as a divorce, it is still recommended to revisit your living will and update it.

Healthcare Power of Attorney

Along with your living will, you must also appoint someone as your healthcare power of attorney or agent (or healthcare proxy).

This person will make medical-related decisions on your behalf when you are unable to make it as you are probably under life support, in a coma, or seriously ill.

Your healthcare power of attorney or agent can even be your close family member, but in the next section, you will learn more about how you should appoint one.

The Importance of Clarity

When proceeding a create your health care directive, it is important to understand that there needs to be clarity when outlining them.

We are all human and can take risks in making medical decisions that can either lead to harmony or potential consequences.

For you to have peace of mind, your health care directive should *clearly* outline what you need and what you don't need.

I have heard of some who include "Do Not Resuscitate" (DNR) and "Do Not Intubate" (DNI) orders in their living will and the doctor follows exactly what was stated and puts it in their medical record.

This is one example that may seem confusing when you read it for the first time but that's the significance of having a clear health care directive. People want to leave the world on their terms and also have religious and cultural beliefs tied to their choices.

Creating Your Directive

In this section, you will learn how to create your directive and have it in full effect when you unexpectedly fall ill or require medical attention.

First and foremost, your directive should be in writing and respective states may have various forms or legal requirements when creating this document.

However, follow this process to ensure your advance directive is ready—starting with your living will:

Outlining Your Medical Wishes

Your living will should clearly outline your medical wishes. Usually, if you have a doctor you know well, you can seek advice from them to know what medical care needs to be addressed when approaching an "end-of-life" situation.

However, the most common medical decisions you should address and make clear are the following:

- Whether you want to receive Cardiopulmonary resuscitation (CPR) when your heart stops beating.

- Do you wish to be put on life support till you can recover fully?

- Are you okay with having pacemakers or implantable cardioverter-defibrillator (ICD) to help keep your heart beating?

- Do you wish to be put on dialysis if your kidneys no longer function?

- If you are suffering from serious infections, do you require antibiotics to cure them?

- Do you wish to be fed through a tube or not?

- Do you wish to be kept in ventilation if you are suffering from difficulty to breath?

- Do you wish to have comfort care or palliative care?

- Do you wish to donate a specific organ, tissue, or even your whole body?

- Do you prefer to have medical care at home rather than in a hospital?
- Do you wish to include DNR or DNI orders in your living will?
- Other medical needs or wishes.

Outlining your medical wishes clearly in your living will help your healthcare agent follow instructions as you stated and it avoids potential conflicts between family members and also doctors.

When you pursue advanced health care planning, you can even include a document called physician orders for life-sustaining treatment (POLST).

This is applicable in some states, and it is especially needed for those diagnosed with an extremely serious illness or who require special medical attention.

A POLST is like a form where your doctor fills it out while complying with your healthcare directive's contents.

This can be an important addition when you want to deeply discuss your medical needs with a doctor and a POLST can always be with you. Some refer to it as a "prescription" for healthcare professionals and it can be helpful when you're suffering from illness and require specific treatment.

Choosing a Health Care Proxy

Next up, you need to choose the right healthcare proxy or power of attorney to complete your healthcare directive.

In most cases, many end up choosing a close family member to make healthcare decisions for them.

Nevertheless, your healthcare agent should meet with the following criteria:

When choosing your healthcare power of attorney, they have to initially meet some state requirements to be legally appointed as one. This can depend on your state.

It is recommended not to choose a doctor or a medical employee to be your healthcare agent. Moreover, it should be someone (whether it is your family member or friend) that you fully trust and are comfortable discussing medical and end-of-life wishes with them.

Furthermore, you have to account for situations where doctors or family members could go against your medical wishes. This is why having a healthcare agent is important.

You need to choose someone who you can trust to advocate and ensure your medical needs are met exactly like you want them.

Remember that when it comes to the actual real-life situation, your healthcare agent will be under a lot of stress. Therefore, I would always lean towards picking someone who doesn't crack under pressure and makes the right decisions.

Discussing with Family

After you have drafted your living will and appointed your healthcare power of attorney, you will need to have the document and forms signed in front of witnesses and also notarized.

You can choose to have your attorney help you with this if you want. Essentially, you should keep the original document safe with you but also accessible to your healthcare agent, attorney, or family members.

It would be wise to give a copy of it to your healthcare agent and a couple of family members. For added security, you could keep a copy with you when you are traveling and even have some sort of card that shows you have advance directives and the contact number of your healthcare agent.

Speaking of family members, it is vital to not keep this subject in the dark. You should let them know about your healthcare directive in advance—and this means openly sharing your medical wishes.

This allows you to clear potential conflicts and make them understand and agree with your wishes. As a result, it would avoid any indecisiveness or arguments during a real-time situation where you need urgent medical attention or nearing death.

Legal and Ethical Considerations

When drafting your healthcare directive, there are some considerations you need to take into account—specifically, legal and ethical considerations.

State Laws and Regulations

When it comes to legal requirements, it is important to note that state laws govern healthcare directives.

This means you have to check with your respective state where you are making your healthcare directive to know and acquire the forms you need to complete.

It is crucial to comply with your state's laws and regulations to make sure your advance directive is deemed valid. This is usually done by having witnesses see you sign, and also have it notarized as I mentioned earlier.

These laws and legal requirements can differ from state to state. I will provide you with an example for clarity.

Take the state of Virginia. The written advance directive over there should compromise the following:

- A living will that outlines their medical wishes.
- A healthcare agent makes healthcare decisions for them.
- Include an "anatomical gift" after their death.

The anatomical gift basically refers to making an organ or tissue donation. Moreover, an oral advance directive could be paid if the person is terminally ill and has difficulty making a written one.

The legal formalities over there include having the directive signed or listened to by at least two witnesses and there is no need to notarize in that state.

Ethical Dilemmas

Having a directive drafted also means that it can present potential ethical dilemmas.

These can be questions such as: Do you wish to adopt extreme measures to extend your life versus simply maintaining the quality of life?

Or do you go with approving a high-risk surgery that could help keep you alive but compromise your quality of life?

These decisions can be up to you and communicating with your family can help determine some answers.

Donating organs is one subject that can spark some debate and different opinions. Doctors have an ethical responsibility to care for their patients and also address the lengthy organ donor waiting list—especially in the US.

If you are totally for or against donating organs, you have to address your intentions in your advance directive so that health professionals can adhere to it. This once again recalls the importance of clarity!

When your healthcare directive addresses many medical-related issues wherever possible, it provides a clearer picture.

When it comes to those involved around you such as your family, healthcare agent, doctors, and so on, they should respect and show empathy towards your wishes and also the caregivers.

Ensuring Compliance

Lastly, healthcare providers should be aware of your advance directives and agree to your instructions. Your healthcare agent should also comply with your terms.

It is important to provide copies of your advance directive to your healthcare agent, and family members, and also ensure the doctors get to read them.

This helps to remove confusion and ensure they respect your wishes.

A healthcare directive is your emergency plan that outlines your medical wishes and should be an integral part of your estate plan.

We have addressed your health needs during a time when you cannot make important decisions. But who will make financial decisions on your behalf?

Beyond health, financial powers of attorney play a crucial role in estate planning and the next chapter will be dedicated to that.

Chapter 6:

Financial Powers of Attorney

Picture yourself in a scenario similar to Mr. Collins. Luckily, you have a healthcare agent to make medical decisions on your behalf.

But unfortunately, you are in a coma or in a state where you cannot make other important decisions anymore. You are put into intensive care at a time when you have significant financial matters to deal with.

These matters can include some outstanding business interests that need looking into, potential investments that you recently acquired but not added to your trust, or a particular asset that you probably want to sell.

There are a lot of important financial decisions to make but sadly, you cannot make them. What to do in these situations? Who will make these decisions for you?

This is where having a financial power of attorney comes to your aid. They will make important financial decisions on your behalf and they are another integral piece to your estate planning.

In this chapter, I will guide you to secure your financial future by appointing a trusted financial power of attorney, understanding their role in managing financial affairs, and also some common mistakes that you can avoid in the process.

The Role of Financial Powers of Attorney

In simple words, a financial power of attorney is a part of your estate plan that grants you legal authority to appoint someone to be in charge of your financial affairs.

This person also referred to as your Attorney-in-Fact, will step in when you need them and make important financial decisions on your behalf.

What exactly are these financial decisions or responsibilities you may wonder?

Well, this can depend on what duties you want your financial power of attorney to take on but here is a list of some of them:

- Executing banking transactions
- Writing checks or paying bills and other expenses
- Managing your investments, assets, and properties
- Managing and executing estate-related transactions

- Updating beneficiaries

- Managing business-related operations

- Making transactions into your Trust

- Donating charitable gifts

- Collaborating with your accountant, investment advisors, or IRS

- Addressing tax-related issues and filing tax returns

- Managing government-related benefits such as Medicare or SS

- Addressing your retirement benefits

- Keeping funds safe in deposit boxes

And the list goes on...

Essentially, your financial power of attorney can take care of all of your important financial responsibilities when you are unable to do and this can be a powerful back-up option to have to manage your estate planning.

They ensure that your financial wishes are respected, and help to prevent financial problems or court intervention—which can be a long and expensive scenario.

Durable vs. Springing Powers

Before selecting your financial power of attorney, you have two major types to choose from—a durable power of attorney or a springing power of attorney.

Clearly, this will depend on your life situation and the complexity of your finances. However, it is good to know the pros and cons of both.

A durable power of attorney—once legally executed—makes the document effective straightaway. This means your agent is going to have legal authority to make decisions on your behalf whether or not you ever become incapacitated.

It is also important to distinguish between incapacitation and death. Being incapacitated is a way of saying that your brain has lost the ability to mentally make decisions—this can include when you are unconscious or terminally ill.

Any power of attorney document is effective till your death. Hence, powers of attorney only serve you till you pass away.

Your durable power of attorney can make decisions on your behalf as long as the document is effective and in any situation. This provides a huge advantage for you.

One major drawback that many people worry about is that since a durable power of attorney gives legal authority and access to your finances immediately, this also brings the question of whether would they abuse the power for their selfish interests.

This is why it is essential to choose someone who you trust for this role.

On the other hand, a springing power of attorney becomes effective under certain "conditions" you state in the document. This means the power of attorney is considered inactive and will only be active to make decisions on your behalf once you become incapacitated.

This is a pro when you only want the POA to act when you need them in extreme conditions but there is a big con. The document has to clearly outline what the conditions are to make sure your POA becomes active.

On top of that, you might need a couple of doctors to provide certification that proves that you are mentally capable of making decisions. This can lead to various dilemmas with the court to legally point your springing power of attorney. Hence, few choose this route and often choose a durable power of attorney.

Selecting an Agent

When selecting your financial agent, it is important to select a person whom you can trust your finances with.

Indeed, the person has to be an adult and it can be anyone—from an attorney to your close family member.

When selecting the right agent, consider their trustworthiness, reliability, and also their competence in handling financial matters.

And most importantly, consider someone who also is willing to be open-minded and consider your viewpoints and other people's.

This is crucial so that your financial power of attorney doesn't lead to the path of abusing the power and making decisions that are not aligned with your goals and values.

Defining Scope and Authority

When preparing a financial power of attorney, you must clearly state what financial responsibilities and decisions your agent is authorized to execute on your behalf.

This is mainly done for transparency and avoiding confusion in your agent's role. Earlier I have mentioned a list of financial duties a POA can be responsible for, so you can use that as a starting point.

Of course, it depends on your finances and the duties you need to take care of usually.

Let's look at a real-life scenario to understand how this can be extremely useful.

Suppose you appoint your brother as your durable financial power of attorney. You got a new job that requires you to migrate to Australia for a couple of years. You have a few financial matters that you will be unable to take care of since you won't be around.

You have a rental property that requires regular checking on tenants and receiving payments every month and also takes care of other miscellaneous tasks related to it such as insurance payments, maintenance, property taxes, and so on.

This means your brother can step in and take care of all of these tasks on your behalf while you are away in Australia.

Then, during your time overseas, let's say you encountered a severe accident and ended up being in a coma. Since your brother is a "durable" POA, this means he can continue carrying out your financial matters despite if you become permanently incompetent in making financial decisions.

This is an example that is illustrated by clearly defining the scope and authority your POA can have and the conditions in which they can continue assisting you and managing your finances on your behalf.

This helps you to not hinder your estate planning progress due to some unfortunate personal circumstances and ensures your loved ones will have enough estate left for them.

Setting Up Your Power of Attorney

Let's look at how you can set up your financial power of attorney. Even if you have a smaller or non-complex estate, you still would require someone to make necessary financial decisions if you were to become incapacitated.

Planning for the future by having a power of attorney can help minimize complications related to your finances.

The ideal way to go about this is to assess your needs first and then determine if you require a durable or springing power of attorney.

After you have determined that, stick to the following procedures when setting up your POA:

Legal Requirements

Legal requirements for enforcing a valid power of attorney can differ from state to state. This should be the first step in part of your research.

Look up your respective state and contact them to learn the legal procedures. You can also get help from your attorney regarding this step. Normally, setting up your POA involves utilizing state-specific forms.

The document itself needs to be dated, define duties the agent can make on your behalf, certain limitations on their role, conditions of when it becomes effective, and finally, have it signed by you.

It requires a witness (or witnesses) to be present when you are signing the document. Also, some states may ask to have it notarized.

Communicating with Your Agent

Drafting the power of attorney document should not be your only job. You should also communicate with your designated agent about the expectations of their role.

This can be important to remove confusion, clear doubts, and provide sufficient information regarding how they can access your finances.

Make your agent understand your financial values, what you prefer, and what you don't. This helps to make sure they are on the same page as you and respect your ideals.

Spend some time having detailed discussions about your estate, various investments, and anything regarding how you want financial matters to be handled diligently.

Incorporating into Your Estate Plan

Finally, integrate your financial POA with your estate plan. This is to ensure you have seamless management of affairs.

You would have already appointed an executor for your will and have trusts step up to manage some or an entire portion of your estate. Hence, it is crucial to integrate your financial agent and have them know the other parties' roles in your estate planning.

Just like when managing wills or trusts, you need to periodically review your financial power of attorney to ensure their duties and conditions are aligned with your needs.

This is crucial to revisit after each significant change in your financial situation or even major life situations. Don't leave your financial power of attorney untouched for many years.

Revisit the document every once a year and compare if circumstances have changed. This can help you to update it and even change your agent if you want to.

We will dive deep into this in the following section where you will get to know how you can avoid a few common mistakes when you appoint a power of attorney.

Avoiding Common Mistakes

Errors can lead to potential consequences down the line. One common mistake is not allowing a professional to review the POA document that you draft.

Remember that it is a legal document and having someone like your attorney beside you when preparing and reviewing it can make a valid POA that aligns with your wishes.

Besides that, here are some more mistakes that one can be prone to if not careful when they appoint an agent:

Overly Broad Powers

Grating your financial power of attorney too much power can be an area of concern. A "general" POA legally authorizes your agent to get into any decisions or transactions without limitations.

These risks can include selling any of your assets without your awareness or even piling up debt for you. This is why the need for a "limited" POA comes of significance so that you can define conditions and limitations in which they can act.

Sometimes, errors can often come from other reasons. For instance, some accidentally give their power of attorney joint ownership of their bank account or business—thinking that would help them make decisions on your behalf.

But this is a terrible mistake and one should distinguish between joint ownership and being a POA.

On the contrary, giving way too little authority can also backfire on the purpose of having a durable POA during the times when you really need it.

Hence, you will need to sit down with your attorney and understand the conditions and limitations you can set, so that you can make a comprehensive POA. Indeed, none of this would matter if your agent is the most trustworthy individual to you but it is still important to consider.

Failing to Update

Another mistake you could make is failing to update your POA or even revoking it when you need it.

I have seen spouses appointing a POA to have peace of mind about their financials. But when a major change in the family situation such as a divorce happens, they fail to update their POA.

The failure to update or revoke your POA doesn't need to be about when a divorce or separation happens. It can be related to your business if your POA makes a lot of business decisions on your behalf and for other purposes.

Moreover, things can change if you fast forward a few years. Consider your agent. You may trust him or her today wholeheartedly. But in a few years, they could entirely change as a person and you may even doubt their integrity.

This is why reviewing and updating your POA shouldn't be ignored.

Not Having Alternate Agents

Mistakes can happen and that is naming the wrong person to be your agent. You can immediately sense it from first impression or could be evident after they make a major bad decision.

You should have alternate agents in line to replace your existing agents if they are not capable of fulfilling their job, or suffer from mental illness, or even death.

Remember that it is your legal and financial life that is on the line, and having reliable, trustworthy, and competent agents can help you in the long term.

Let's wrap up what you have learned so far:

Wills? Check.

Trusts? Check.

Advanced Healthcare Directives? Check.

Powers of Attorney? Check.

Now that you have solid legal documents as part of your estate plan, let's shift our attention to managing and protecting your valuable assets.

Chapter 7:

Asset Management and Protection

Visualize you have everything in your estate plan in order. You have a comprehensively written will, a trust set up, and your health care directive and powers of attorney sorted out.

Yet, the families of the deceased still end up getting into estate complications. One common reason is tied down to the mismanagement of assets.

Examples of such mismanagement can include not knowing where exactly these assets are located, not having access to the deceased's online accounts, and having assets that don't have any designated beneficiaries.

Mistakes can happen as we are all human but this chapter will help you to assess, organize, and protect your assets. Thus, ensuring its growth and preservation for future generations.

Assessing and Organizing Assets

The consequences of failing to organize your assets can often lead to expensive procedures and losses for your family.

There are incidents where families couldn't claim insurance policies, bank accounts, and even real estate. Hence, it ends up going to the state government.

The first step that you can take is to spend time and assess all of the assets you have acquired during your time.

The following steps will show you how you can organize your assets to enhance your estate plan's robustness:

Inventory of Assets

Taking an inventory of your assets is usually the first step before you draft your will, but we will once again, go through its importance.

Having an inventory helps you to organize your assets and understand each asset's value.

Make sure your inventory list consists of *both* tangible and intangible assets.

For example, these can be your tangible assets:

- your home
- other real estate properties

- land
- vehicles
- household furniture
- jewelry
- clothing and accessories
- art collections
- coins
- books
- antiques
- any other tangible or physical items that have some value

Whereas, examples of your intangible assets can include:

- life insurance policies (yes, it's considered as an asset)
- 401(k)s, IRAs, or other retirement plans
- bank accounts such as savings, checkings, CDs, etc.
- stocks and mutual funds
- bonds or annuities
- ownership or a share in a business
- intellectual property such as copyrights, trademarks or patents
- any other intangible or invisible items that have some value

Of course, we have learned earlier that even making a list of debts such as mortgages, loans, and credit card debt is typically part of knowing your estate's value.

Valuation and Documentation

The next step is to assess the value of each asset and keep up-to-date documentation of each. For example, this could be in the form of deeds or titles for real estate properties, and even appraisal reports for some of your assets.

Valuation and documentation are crucial steps in organizing your assets for estate planning and tax purposes.

For instance, if you have one property located in the US or even in foreign countries, you have to determine the current market value of it and this would be added to your estate's value.

Imagine situations where failing to account for them can lead to creditors getting paid from other assets that should've been left to your family or your family not being able to benefit from the asset's value for their benefit.

Another important point is that you should inform your family or loved ones about what they need to know about specific assets. These can be simple matters such as if they know which banks you have accounts, where your safety deposit box is located and how it can be accessed, and passwords to certain online accounts.

Ensure all of your assets have a beneficiary designation and even a contingency beneficiary. Take note of them and update them regularly whenever you need to.

Digital Asset Management

Since this is a modern-day guide, it should be noted that you should include digital assets in your inventory.

These assets could include all of your online accounts, social media accounts, and even cryptocurrency.

To stay digitally organized, include details on how to access them and include them in your estate plan. We will dive deep into this later in the chapter.

Protecting Your Assets

Asset protection planning should be a top priority in your estate planning. Our loved ones are important to us and taking that extra step to shield respective assets could do favors in preserving them for your family and keeping them away from creditors.

Creditors only think about money after you pass away. The executor has the fiduciary duty to notify creditors regarding your death so that they can make claims.

To avoid creditors from claiming assets that are very important to you and your loved ones such as your family home, business, vehicles, and so on, you need to activate a robust asset-protection plan.

This can include utilizing any of the following options:

Insurance Strategies

The first option includes making use of insurance policies such as life insurance, liability insurance, property insurance, etc.

This can help protect your assets from events of uncertainty, especially when you prepare your estate plan in advance. A lot can happen to your assets until the day you move on from this world.

One major insurance strategy is to have a life insurance policy that can provide an adequate financial buffer to your family after you pass away.

Of course, there are many other ways in which you can do without insurance policies.

For instance, you can make use of "transfer on death" deeds for real estate properties or certain assets. This helps to transfer assets immediately to your family after your death. You must check with your respective state regarding this.

To minimize paying taxes, many opt for the strategy of gifting certain assets to their loved ones before they die. Especially if the gift is not above a certain threshold limit, there can be a gift tax exemption. Moreover, it helps to preserve assets from your creditors.

Liability Considerations

Another way of making sure you protect your assets from creditors is to minimize your "personal liability." This is pretty much explainable if you have a business. If not, here's a bit of context: When your creditors can touch your personal assets, then there's personal liability involved.

In businesses such as sole proprietorships, this happens. When that particular business piles up debts, creditors can seize the sole proprietor's assets. In such a situation, there's personal liability.

However, business legal structures such as a limited liability company (LLC) or a family limited partnership (FLP), provide a firm legal wall that separates business assets and personal assets.

How can this be integrated into your estate planning, you may wonder?

For example, you can own a piece of your rental property through an LLC as a means to shield that asset from potential lawsuits. Because, on this occasion, your rental property is a "business asset."

Likewise, business creditors can only touch business assets and not your personal assets if you have an LLC. Hence, you will need to do some comprehensive planning with your assets in case you have a business.

You can always establish a separate LLC to shield your assets too.

An FLP is more of a family-owned business where it can protect your assets since family members and spouses own a small portion of the partnership—meaning they have control over the partnership's assets.

Asset Protection Trusts

Another effective option you can utilize is to set up trusts. You have learned in its dedicated chapter how trusts can be effective in protecting assets from creditors—especially irrevocable ones.

Irrevocable trusts ensure assets are protected from creditors because you no longer own those assets. After all, it was permanently transferred to the trust's ownership.

There are two kinds of asset protection trusts: one set up within the country (in the US) and offshore asset protection trusts.

You can choose either setup according to your liking. I have seen a few going with offshore asset protection trusts because they provide an "extra" protection so that creditors won't be able to claim them.

Other reasons why they opt for offshore trusts are because they own a couple of properties outside the US, and some foreign jurisdictions have favorable regulations and tax laws.

According to those reasons, it seems to make sense to have it established in a foreign country. Some trending foreign jurisdictions that you can explore if you are interested in setting up offshore trusts include the Bahamas, Belize, Bermuda, Cayman Islands, Cook Islands, Cyprus, Singapore, and the United Kingdom.

Digital Asset, Cryptocurrency and Cyber Insurance

Organizing digital assets is also a crucial part of your estate planning. Some even refer to it as organizing a "digital estate plan."

The purpose of organizing your digital assets is to make sure your loved ones can locate and access these online accounts or digital assets.

There can be digital assets or properties that may have significant financial value and also this could be considered to have it go through probate.

Additionally, with many identity theft and cybercrime happening online, it is crucial to have these digital assets in the custody of your loved ones.

The following shows what digital assets you need to account for when making a digital estate plan.

Inventory and Valuation

Just like we learned earlier when making an asset inventory list, this time create a detailed inventory of all your digital assets.

Account for everything you have, even if it may seem it doesn't have any financial value. Take note of all of your digital files stored in your PC, and cloud databases. Also take note of all of your online accounts, social media accounts, and cryptocurrency holdings.

After compiling the list, assess their current value and also analyze their potential future value—this can be particularly seen with digital currencies due to their volatility.

For instance, keep a separate list or record of your cryptocurrency wallets and their contents. Have it stored safely and keep an up-to-date record of it with access keys if applicable.

You can repeat the procedure with other digital assets such as online business assets, digital collectibles, and other digital assets of sentimental value.

Estate Planning for Cryptocurrency

If you own cryptocurrency, ensure to include them in your estate plan. Outline instructions clearly on how to access and manage them.

You also need to decide who will inherit so-and-so digital currencies. You can include private keys and other instructions for the beneficiary.

Moreover, you can include other specific wishes related to when they inherit the digital currency or asset. These can be instructions to either keep assets such as non-fungible tokens (NFTs) or sell them at a future date.

It can depend on who you would want to leave your cryptocurrency with, but it should be someone you trust and also a tech-savvy individual.

They should be able to comprehend detailed instructions regarding wallet passwords, key storage location, and so on, so they can successfully access and manage these digital assets according to your best wishes.

Cyber Insurance

When it comes to protecting your digitally-owned assets against cyber-related threats, you can consider cyber insurance.

With hacking and theft being common in the digital world, it is not inconceivable to think that your digital assets could be exposed to thieves out there.

Cyber insurance helps by providing coverage for financial losses that result from these so-called cyber attacks on your digital assets.

Just like how you select a regular life insurance policy, you may want to consider certain factors such as its coverage limits and also the conditions at which the coverage gets activated.

For instance, check if it covers risks such as data breaches that result in devaluation of your digital asset, theft of your digital currency, etc.

This is an extra measure you can take to provide an added layer of security to your digital assets in the worst-case scenario so that your family won't be affected financially by its loss.

Strategies for Growth and Preservation

Your assets deserve to be preserved not only from creditors but also allow them to appreciate.

Certain assets can provide life-long financial support to your family after your time.

For instance, properties are powerful assets where that can appreciate in value and also allow your loved ones to make recurring income from them when they use them responsibly.

Nevertheless, there are other strategies you can consider for protecting your assets:

Investment Strategies

Put the hat of an investor—like Warren Buffet. How is he so successful in investing, besides investing in high-growth stocks?

He also diversifies his investment portfolio.

You too, should look to prioritize this strategy and develop a diversified investment portfolio.

Your portfolio should look to minimize risk tolerance and also benefit achieving your long-term financial goals.

A good rule of thumb is to balance all of your asset allocations in your portfolio. Review your stocks, bonds, and real estate investments, and consider how you can achieve a mix of growth and income for your portfolios.

Why do you think the rich keep getting rich and are safe from external crises such as inflation or recession? Because they split their wealth into different assets: They keep cash, stocks, bonds, properties, cryptocurrencies, and even own land, minerals, and precious metals.

Do you see how diversified their portfolio looks?

A method known as portfolio rebalancing can help you to regularly review your portfolio and adjust investments or asset allocations according to your financial goals.

You can use this as a way to add certain assets that you may have not owned or even remove assets that are not providing significant monetary value for you.

Make it a habit to practice portfolio rebalancing periodically with your portfolio and within a few years, you will see how you create a diversified investment portfolio that can benefit your loved ones and future generations.

Succession Planning

For your business or investments, planning for the future is a crucial step.

Succession planning helps ensure a smooth transition of its ownership to successors such as your family members or any other individual you name.

A succession plan includes providing a clear overview of transferring ownership and its control.

For a family-owned business, many make use of buy-sell agreements. This is an agreement that allows existing partners in the business to purchase shares of a partner who passed away.

Succession planning is key when you have businesses so that their growth won't get affected despite your death.

Charitable Giving

Lastly, for the betterment of society, you can include charitable giving in your estate plan.

Many not only do this to fulfill their philanthropic goals but also to maximize certain tax benefits. You will learn more about this particular tax benefit in detail in the next chapter.

There are many ways in which you can give your assets to charity.

Some directly donate assets to a charity for starters. Others set up charitable trusts as they can help donate portions of your estate to your favorite charity, while also reducing your estate's taxable value.

The common types of charitable trusts that you should know about are Charitable Lead Trust (CLT) and Charitable Remainder Trust (CRT). You may have recalled me mentioning them when we discussed specific types of trusts.

The difference between the two is down to how they both work.

CLTs help transfer your assets to the trust and your favorite charity will receive income or annuities from the trust for a fixed term. After that term or your death, the remaining assets will be passed to your beneficiaries and not the charity.

On the other hand, CRTs are the opposite. You can set up the trust and have it pay income or annuities to you or your family for a fixed term. After that term or your death, the remaining assets will go to your favorite charity. Do you see the contrast?

Including a plan to give away your assets to a charity or a cause you fully support can be important to you, provide a great feeling, and can leave a mark on the world.

You got your will sorted, your trust set up, your powers of attorney appointed, and all of your assets protected.

So, what next?

Effective estate planning also requires a good understanding and planning for taxes.

Chapter 8:

Estate Planning and Taxes

One cannot escape taxes even after death.

This statement often surprises many. Typically during probate, your executor will be asked to file your "final" tax return and pay the remaining taxes you owe.

We all know about the saying that death and taxes are a certainty in *life,* but taxes after *death?* Might sound ridiculous at first but it does make sense when you think about it.

Regardless, you don't need to worry too much about taxes if you understand the types of estate-related taxes involved and navigate the complexities with effective tax planning strategies.

This chapter will help you understand that there is tax exemption when accounting for estate taxes and to be frank, paying estate taxes depends on where you live in the U.S.

Curious to learn more?

Estate and Inheritance Taxes

First and foremost, there are two major types of taxes that you should know about when conducting your estate planning—estate taxes and inheritance taxes.

Many often get confused with the difference between the two but I will explain it in simple words.

Estate taxes—also referred to as wealth transfer tax or death tax—are imposed on the deceased's estate. This is often paid from the estate itself and is usually settled by your executor or personal representative using Form 706.

Whereas, inheritance taxes are imposed on the assets, funds, or "inheritance" the beneficiary receives from your estate. In other words, the beneficiary has to file and pay for inheritance taxes.

Federal and State Taxes

If you are especially based in the US, an interesting fact is that not all states impose estate taxes or inheritance taxes. For instance, there are about 17 states that impose either estate taxes or inheritance taxes.

States that impose estate taxes include Connecticut, Hawaii, Illinois, Maine, Massachusetts, Minnesota, New York, Oregon, Rhode Island, Vermont, and Washington (*Inheritance tax vs estate tax,* n.d.).

Only a few states impose inheritance taxes. This includes Iowa, Kentucky, Nebraska, New Jersey, and Pennsylvania (*Inheritance tax vs estate tax,* n.d.).

Only Maryland imposes both estate and inheritance taxes. While remaining states like Arizona, California, Delaware, Florida, Ohio, Texas, and so on impose neither.

When you compare the two taxes, estate taxes generally have higher tax rates and also exemption thresholds. For context, according to the IRS website for unified tax rates, an asset or transfer that's up to only $10,000 in value, has about an 18% tax rate. Whereas, for over $1 million, the tax rate can go up to 40% (*Instructions for Form 706 | Internal Revenue Service,* 2018).

Exemption amounts can vary from state to state and also according to the updated exemption amounts (usually you can refer to by visiting the IRS website).

For example, according to 2024 exemption amounts, Massachusetts allows up to $2 million. Meanwhile, Connecticut's exemption amount is up to $13.61 million (*State Death Tax Chart,* n.d.).

Let's use a simple example to illustrate the estate taxes one can owe. For instance, if your total estate value is $10 million and the exemption is allowed till $13.61 million, that means your taxable estate is zero and you owe no taxes.

However, if your total estate value is $15.61 million, this means your first $13.61 million is exempted and the remaining $2 million ($15.61 million - $13.61 million) is considered taxable estate.

As a result of the 40% tax rate, you would owe around $800,000 in estate taxes. See how simple it is? Nothing complicated here.

Inheritance tax exemptions are usually accounted for if you transfer wealth to an immediate family member. For instance, your spouse wouldn't definitely need to pay inheritance taxes, while your children most likely wouldn't need to as well. Anyone outside that will be subjected to inheritance taxes depending on the state they reside in.

Even transferring wealth to your grandchildren can have a certain tax imposed called a generation-skipping transfer tax (GSTT). This happens when you "skip" a generation or two when you transfer some of your inheritance. So, this type of tax should also be kept at the back of your mind.

Taxable Assets

After understanding the difference between estate taxes and inheritance taxes, you can focus on identifying which assets in your estate could be potentially subjected to taxes.

What are these assets to be precise? These can include your home, other real estate, cash, stocks, bonds, retirement accounts, and personal belongings such as cars, clothing, and household items.

Life insurance coverage is usually tax-free. However, the IRS considers the interest in life insurance policies or annuities taxable.

When your beneficiaries need to account for inheritance taxes, it depends on various factors such as the size of the estate or inheritance they received and tax regulations in their state. Also, as I mentioned just a while back, it can depend on the relationship with the deceased. They may not owe inheritance tax if they are an immediate family member.

Using a simple example, suppose you leave $10 million to your spouse. According to the state laws, let's say it charges a 10% tax rate on inheritance that exceeds $3 million.

Since it is your spouse, they don't need to pay any inheritance tax. But if you decided to leave the $10 million to a distant relative or best friend, then that beneficiary should pay inheritance taxes on the $7 million (since $10 million - $3 million). Thus, the tax they owe would be around $700,000 (10% of $7 million). Clear?

Besides inheritance taxes, your beneficiaries may need to watch out for capital gains taxes after they inherit certain assets that appreciate. For instance, you might leave a property that's worth $1,500,000 to your son or daughter. If they sell the home later for $2,000,000, then they have to pay capital gains tax for the $500,000 profit.

Minimizing Tax Burden

To minimize your tax liability, you will need to employ strategies regularly to reduce the taxable amounts your estate or your beneficiaries owe.

Many often utilize the following strategies such as gifting assets annually within the specified IRS threshold limit so that it helps to reduce taxable estate frequently.

Gifting everything all at once is not a wise strategy as this can lead to breaking the threshold limit, and you can be subjected to "gift taxes."

Keep in mind that you can gift assets to a charity of your choice as well. Besides giving away assets, you can also shield these assets in irrevocable trusts as it helps to reduce taxable estate.

You probably must be wondering, but "Wait, Zachary! You just told me that not all states impose estate taxes, so why can't I relocate them to those states?"

If you did give serious thought to that, then it shows you understand how you can minimize tax liability. And yes! You can also move your assets to a state with favorable tax regulations or no estate taxes levied.

However, there can be some drawbacks, well, logistically speaking. The major part of your estate plan is centered around the state you live in and most likely to pass away there. You have important people like your attorney, executor, trustee, beneficiaries, and so on.

Therefore, you will need to plan how you can ensure your beneficiaries can get their inheritance with ease and make them travel halfway across the country which can often lead to inconvenience and potential conflicts.

Tax Planning Strategies

In this section, I will walk you through several tax planning strategies that you can employ to minimize your estate tax burden.

These options can be helpful to have when you are considering ways to reduce tax liability and how it can be tailored specifically to your estate planning goals.

Gifting Assets

As we have learned earlier in the chapter, gifting your assets can be a really good option. You can take advantage of annual gift tax exemptions or lifetime gift exemptions to minimize tax liability, At the same time, it helps you to successfully transfer wealth to your respective heirs "tax-free."

Even if your heirs live in a state that imposes inheritance tax, they wouldn't need to pay such taxes because they received it as a gift.

The wise strategy you can implement here is to gift assets up to an annual limit to multiple beneficiaries every year.

Make a separate plan for this so that you have a good idea of what these assets are and how much they reduce your taxable estate without incurring gift taxes.

For clarity, as of 2023, the annual gift tax exclusion is up to $17,000 per gift or donation (*Instructions for Form 706 | Internal Revenue Service,* 2018). As a result, you can gift up to $17,000 in cash or assets to people every year, while not going above the annual threshold limit.

If you are planning to gift assets to minors, you can also avoid incurring gift taxes by using custodial accounts and executing the transaction under the Uniform Transfers to Minors Act (UTMA).

UTMA is often regulated by your respective state laws. It allows minors to receive any real asset you give, which can include cash, real estate, and securities, among others.

Trusts and Tax Implications

Utilize specific trusts to spread assets and also reduce your taxable estate. The various types of trusts that can help you with this are as follows:

- **Irrevocable Life Insurance Trust (ILIT):** This is a type of irrevocable trust that stores life insurance policies. This trust helps insure your beneficiaries by paying out the proceeds tax-free.

- **Marital Trusts:** This includes AB trusts and Qualified Terminable Interest Property (QTIP) trusts. They can benefit surviving spouses, immediate family members, and other beneficiaries. AB trusts allow a surviving spouse to receive interest from the trust, while QTIP trust limits such access.

- **Qualified Personal Residence Trust (QPRT):** For situations such as transferring your home to your spouse, you can make use of QPRT for tax benefits and also you can continue living in the house for a fixed period regardless of transferring it under the trust's name.

The above three are some of the most effective and commonly opted trusts that can help if you are mainly prioritizing reducing tax liability. However, other irrevocable trusts can help you do the same, but you should always stay updated with the trust's terms and state tax laws.

Your attorney, for example, can help with providing more insights regarding updated tax regulations when you are setting up trusts for minimizing taxable estate.

Charitable Donations

Another effective way to minimize tax burden or taxable estate is to make charitable donations.

You can make use of the two charitable trusts—Charitable Lead Trust (CLT) and Charitable Remainder Trust (CRT). We have covered how they both work in the previous chapter. You can utilize either of the two trusts depending on your financial circumstances and estate planning goals.

Charitable donations should be right up your alley when you want to fulfill your philanthropic goals and also reduce estate taxes at the same time.

You can also choose to donate appreciated assets that you have kept for a long time such as stocks, mutual funds, bonds, etc. so that you don't even need to pay capital gains tax for it and instead, contribute to your favorite charity.

To summarize what we have learned from the previous chapters, you can minimize your tax burden or taxable estate by

- gifting assets before you die.
- setting up trusts.
- giving assets away to charity.
- establishing a FLP.

With the above strategies, even if you live in a state that imposes federal estate taxes, you can most likely avoid owing any taxes if you regularly reduce your estate value so that it doesn't exceed the exemption amount.

Working with Tax Professionals

The point of this chapter is not just to educate you regarding the taxes you need to plan for when you conduct your estate planning but also to understand the importance of seeking professional help.

If you can do tax planning all by yourself because you have a background in this field or have sufficient experience doing so, then go for it!

If not, I would recommend having professionals guide you toward making the best tax-planning decisions wherever you can.

Finding the Right Advisor

Choosing a tax professional or an estate planning attorney may sound intimidating at first. But there is a lot of demand for such professionals and their experience brings more value to the table.

You need to look for professionals who are specialists in optimizing for tax efficiency. One good way to look at it is to assess their academic background and identify credentials such as Legum Magister in Taxation Law (LLM) or Certified Public Accountant (CPA).

Besides qualifications, study if they have sufficient social proof or success stories of clients they have worked with. This is crucial as you would want someone who has experience in producing results for previous estate planners.

Furthermore, they should be compatible to work with as you need to maintain relationships with them for the long term.

Regular Tax Reviews

After appointing your tax professional or accountant, schedule your tax review cycles. This can be scheduled annually or bi-annually depending on how often you would like to change your estate plan and respond to changes in tax regulations.

You may even call for tax reviews with your professional advisor in case there is a sudden change in your financial situation or estate planning goals.

If you ever encounter such situations in the future, never put them off for months or years and immediately address them so you can benefit from maximum tax efficiency with the help and guidance of tax professionals.

Staying Informed on Tax Laws

Tax advisors, accounts, or estate planning attorneys are always informed about the current tax laws. Yes, they charge for their services and it can be pretty expensive, but focus on the value they can provide to you.

Most get intimidated by maintaining their tax-planning strategies because they find it difficult to keep up with current tax laws and find tasks such as accounting taxable estate and so on mundane.

Keeping a network of tax professionals opens up a source where you can gain information and stay updated with changes in federal and state tax regulations that may or may not impact your estate plan.

For instance, I have recently heard that the state of Iowa may look to remove the inheritance tax completely by 2025. This could impact you in case you are residing in Iowa and can aid in future tax planning purposes.

One subtle change in tax regulations may open up an opportunity for you to maximize tax efficiency or mitigate some potential adverse tax consequences.

In addition, this may also lead to you revisiting your estate plan and making necessary adjustments to your estate planning strategy.

As we wrap up the chapter regarding taxes, you have mastered the fundamentals 7 steps for making a clear and effective estate plan.

To summarize, you have

1. assessed your estate planning needs.
2. created a comprehensive will.
3. set up trusts.
4. created advanced healthcare directives.
5. appointed powers of attorney.
6. implemented strategies to protect and manage assets.
7. employed efficient tax-planning strategies.

You are starting to see your plan taking shape.

Let's make sure it stays relevant over time and in the next chapter, you will learn how you can maintain your estate plan effectively.

Chapter 9:

Updating and Maintaining Your Estate Plan

So, you have made your perfect estate plan and put it into action. What else can go wrong after what we have discussed so far?

Oh, yes. There is this ONE thing!

People end up creating their estate plan only *once* and forget about the whole thing for years—a mistake that you should humbly avoid.

Picture that you made your estate plan and fast forward a few years, a new child is introduced to your family.

Your estate plan already covers for your other children but not for the new child. As a result, this sparks a need to update it.

But the birth of a child isn't the only reason why you need to update your estate plan. This chapter will walk you through when and how you can update your estate plan to ensure it stays relevant.

Don't let the dynamic nature of your life ruin your estate plans. Embrace it!

Reviewing Your Estate Plan

Reviewing your estate plan can be overlooked because it can sometimes feel redundant or overwhelming to go through pages of your plan. But don't make a mistake—it is your plan and your life!

One should take responsibility for reviewing their estate plan regularly so that they or their family don't regret the potential consequences in the future if it is left not updated according to present-day relevance.

Here are a few steps and indications you can consider to have a system in place so that you understand the need to review your estate plan:

Regular Check-Ups

Firstly, determine a schedule where you can do regular check-ups on your estate plan. This involves reviewing them, reflecting on your current life situation and family dynamics, and updating them accordingly.

You can determine the schedule as per your liking. You can set an annual review where you reflect on your estate plan every year or make it once every five years or so.

If you are doing annual check-ups, arrange a yearly meeting with your estate planning attorney for more guidance regarding keeping up-to-date with current estate tax laws or other current affairs.

Responding to Life Changes

You must also respond to major life changes or events along with your regular check-up schedule. This should be a trigger that makes you immediately think about looking up your estate plan, reviewing it, and updating it if needed.

What could these major life events, you may wonder? It can be any of the following:

- birth of a child or grandchild
- marriage
- divorce or separation
- death of a beneficiary, executor, or trustee
- change in your financial situation such as receiving more wealth, bankruptcy, opening or closing a business, etc.
- or any other life event that is important to you

Whenever a major life event occurs in your life, it should act as a trigger. For example, let's say you already have an estate plan—with trusts set up to cater to your family's needs.

But a major change happens in your life. You end up divorcing your spouse and get re-married to a new spouse. As a result, this should already set an alarm off in your head that it's time to revisit your estate plan.

You will review it and find out that you may be required to update the terms of your trust so that your ex-spouse won't come claiming your inheritance (a situation that no one would like to happen). Or you may need to add your new spouse as part of your estate plan. This procedure repeats whenever any other major life change occurs in your life.

If you want to recall the need to update your estate plan, you can make use of memorizing the 4 Ds—Divorce, Death, Disability, and Decisions (Yokabitus, 2019).

If you divorce your spouse, update your estate plan. If there is a death of someone named in your will, update your estate plan. If you or someone in your plan suffers from a disability, update your estate plan. If you change your intentions or decisions, then this also means you need to update your estate plan.

Legal Updates

As mentioned earlier about having yearly meetings with your estate planning attorney, it is mostly to stay informed about any changes that can impact your estate plan.

There can be changes in estate law and tax regulations which can provide either an opportunity or threat to your estate plan. Thus, it should be in your best interest to adjust your necessary documents to comply with new and updated laws.

For example, you may encounter one day when there is a change in your state's inheritance tax laws. The tax rate has increased for such and such estate taxable value.

Hence, this requires your immediate action to adjust your estate plan by transferring more assets to a trust to reduce your estate value so that you can minimize taxes or gift them to your loved ones.

Making Necessary Adjustments

Reviewing itself requires a lot of attention to detail and reflecting on your current life situation to identify the adjustments you need to make.

The next part that comes is making those necessary changes. Usually, people only change their state plan but fail to notify interested parties or even reassess their goals.

This could be a big mistake and you should ensure that you don't make such a one-dimensional approach.

One prime example of a one-dimensional way of updating estate plans I have seen is only updating the plan after each major life change.

Even though it is necessary to review and update your estate plan after each life event, it isn't the only indicator to do so.

In this section, you will learn how you can take a proactive approach to be more effective in making adjustments to your estate plan.

Amending Documents

First and foremost, you will need to update your estate plan and you can do this by attaching amendments. For example, codicils for wills or amendments for trusts.

These documents can help you update your will or trust so that it stays aligned with your current wishes.

You can also choose to set up new trusts, transfer assets from an old trust to a new trust (via trust decanting), or craft a new updated will to revoke the older versions.

Other major changes can also include changing an executor or trustee, as you would formally amend the document to make this change happen.

Reassessing Goals and Needs

After making such major adjustments, many fail to reassess their goals and needs according to their current situation.

Remember that your estate planning goals can change from the point you start doing it for the first time to many years later. Hence, it is vital to make your goals stay relevant to your ongoing situation.

You can take a proactive approach by periodically reassessing your financial and family goals. This helps in ensuring your estate plan remains on the same page with your objectives.

Moreover, it helps you to identify new goals or remove goals that have become irrelevant. For example, your financial situation now may not be that great. But a few years later, it may improve and you are building greater wealth.

This provides you more room to include goals such as contributing some of your estate to your favorite charity or bringing in new investments into your estate plan.

In such a situation, you will stay updated with your present-day situation and incorporate incremental goals that help provide more for your family when you include such assets or investments in your estate plan.

Being proactive leads to better changes in your estate planning and this is a necessary mindset to implement—especially when you have an estate plan done and needs to be maintained regularly.

Communicating Changes to Family

After you make the necessary adjustments or changes, you will need to make it a habit to inform your family or any affected parties of these changes.

You don't need to notify every beneficiary but those who might need to know regarding the changes you have made that impact them.

When it comes to your immediate family members or loved ones, they should be kept in the loop. This is necessary to prevent surprises and also ensure everyone is on the same page as you.

If you change your executor or trustee for instance, this needs to be communicated to all of your beneficiaries. If you make changes in picking a different guardian, then the new and former guardian should be notified—along with the minor children and related family members.

Many estate-related conflicts occur after the deceased passes away. This is mainly because the deceased makes certain changes in their estate plan that come as a major surprise to some family members or beneficiaries. As a result, this is what can happen when you don't notify the affected parties of such changes.

Being proactive helps to minimize such severe consequences. Execute a forward-thinking approach of regularly reassessing your goals, making necessary changes, and notifying members of those changes. Thus, your estate settlement will go smoothly.

Ensuring Continuous Relevance

One of the biggest mistakes one can make is doing an estate plan just for the sake of it.

I would look to treat an estate plan like how you would treat your business goals, financial goals, family goals, and so on.

Estate plans are as vital as the other mentioned goals or top priorities. It requires the same nurturing and attention as your other important goals do.

When your child graduates from college, this urges you to reassess your financial goals and family goals. Likewise, it should also urge you to reassess your estate plan and update it to your current life situation.

As you can see, your estate plan is actually integrated with whatever happens in your life. It is equal to your other top priority goals because it is about your life and your family's future!

Long-Term Vision

When planning your estate and legacy, having a long-term vision is a must. But keeping that continuous long-term vision is a different story.

It can be easy to be overwhelmed by life situations (difficult ones especially) so that you end up not showing the same desire to think far ahead as you would usually do.

I was guilty of this when I had to endure a tough time after losing one of my close friends. The event devoured my thoughts daily and I found it difficult to go about with any of my work. This could have been worse if it was one of my family members.

But, I had to keep going and keep my long-term vision by securing my family's future. In a strange way, the tragic loss of my close friend gave me the boost to keep my estate plan updated after his family had to deal with a lot of inheritance complications.

Your circumstances could be different. I shared with you a situation where you can see that it doesn't need to be something related to your estate plan that lets your guard down and affects your long-term thinking.

Our minds can be vulnerable to the simplest of things. It's totally natural. However, your estate plan should keep evolving to support your goals over time.

For instance, if you have a family business and your long-term priority is to preserve it for future generations, then you should be proactive and have clear succession planning. Don't let anything stop you from achieving the objectives that you set.

Having a long-term vision means running a marathon. It requires your mind to stay alert at all times, be flexible in responding to changes, and embrace longevity.

Adapting to New Circumstances

Flexibility is key when you are updating your estate plan to stay aligned with your present-day circumstances.

If you have a change in one of the top life priorities, that is health, wealth, or family, then this requires you to be prepared to adapt to these new circumstances.

I know it's easier said than done. Imagine a new circumstance that pops up out of nowhere, where one is diagnosed with a serious illness or cancer. This is, of course, a type of horrible news that would dampen one's mental health.

Nevertheless, these circumstances should prompt you or anyone to probably update their health care directives or medical power of attorney.

Have a system that helps you to update your estate plan even when mentally draining situations like these could occur and surprise you.

I would look to having an attorney to take care of updating the plan and also have a close family member who you trust to help you adapt to such circumstances by reviewing and updating your estate plan.

Engaging with Professionals

Since I mentioned attorneys, that's where having a network of estate planning professionals can come to your aid. This is a part of your estate plan system that you need to develop.

Maintaining good relationships with professionals such as your attorney, financial planners, tax advisors, etc., can ensure your estate plan benefits from their expert insights and guidance.

Professionals are specialists in their field and that means executing *up-to-date* practices. It might be expensive to regularly consult with professionals. Some charge a lot per session.

But in the grand scheme of things, it is worth it to get guidance into navigating changes in your life and the legal landscape.

With a dynamic estate plan in place with a robust system regularly reviewing it, let's explore how you can effectively pass on your legacy in the next chapter.

Chapter 10:

Legacy Planning and Family Dynamics

Carve your name on hearts, not tombstones. A legacy is etched into the minds of others and the stories they share about you. — Shannon L. Alder (Sweatt, 2016)

Have you thought about how you would like to be remembered after you move on from this world?

Creating a meaningful legacy that reflects your values and fosters harmony is something most look to try prioritizing.

However, the busyness of creating and maintaining an effective estate plan can be challenging. Many tend to forget what is it they want to leave behind after they pass away.

Read through this chapter as you will learn how you can define your legacy, communicate it to your loved ones, and also navigate the intricacies of family dynamics.

Defining Your Legacy

Your estate plan consists of the legal structures, writings, and assets that enable you to provide tangible and intangible support for your loved ones after your death.

But your legacy plan is something personal. It communicates your actions, emotions, and your essence that can be felt and remembered forever by your loved ones—even after death.

We hustle through life by achieving personal goals, creating successful families, and learning valuable life lessons.

But as we complete two-thirds of our lifetime, we start to think about what type of legacy we want to leave behind.

How would I want to be remembered after I die? And how would I exactly define my legacy?

Defining your legacy can be a personal topic. You have to dig deeper into your heart to truly uncover what your truest and deepest intentions are.

To make the process go as smoothly as possible, here are three major factors that you can assess that can help you define your legacy:

Personal Values and Beliefs

The first step is to start from within—the self. Understand what YOU are all about.

What are your core values and beliefs that assisted your life to what it has been now? What of these values do you wish to influence your legacy and how?

Maybe it could be your commitment to self-education. You became successful in your life because you valued the importance of education, and you would want to articulately communicate that value or belief to future generations.

Maybe it could be your discipline to build immense wealth through entrepreneurship.

Or it could be your warmth of giving yourself away to others by helping others and donating to your favorite charity.

This may take some time to find out if you haven't explored this particular phase yet. If you want to explore your deepest values and intentions, firstly, get away from the busy noise.

Take some time off from your usual schedule and wander into the wilderness. Travel. Go into the nature. Calm your mind. Yes, it may sound like a cliché, but it produces effective results.

I personally found mine when I got away from the noise and spent a few weeks traveling. Not only did it help me disconnect from how hectic our life situation can be but also reflect on things that matter to us the most and reevaluate our priorities.

This breakthrough helped me to implement better and more intentional strategies for my estate plan because I defined what type of legacy I want to leave behind for my family and the people I have known for my life.

Family Traditions and Histories

The next step is to go outwards and look immediately at the people around you—notably, your family.

Family traditions and their deep rich history usually shape the person you are today and what you can pass on to your heirs.

There could be family traditions that you may want to preserve and pass down to your heirs.

This could be the way how you were brought up to be a successful person and you would want the same to be replicated by your children and grandchildren.

It could also be family traditions that you want to create or already created that you would want to pass on to future generations.

These could be traditions that you cultivated due to experiencing a challenging childhood or certain difficult periods in your life.

I have a friend who came from a background of strong family traditions. His parents and generations before him took education seriously and nurtured their children by getting them into the best schools and placements at top reputable companies.

Because of such strong family foundations, he planned his estate accordingly to benefit his children and grandchildren. He set aside a large portion of his estate for his children's higher education and set up a trust with college funds that his grandchildren could later use for their education.

He was a man who had a long-term vision and planned his estate according to how he was raised and how he wanted his family and future generations to benefit from rich and moral values.

Similarly, you can identify and plan to preserve your family traditions by passing down values that matter the most to you and how they can enrich your loved ones' lives and most importantly, have a more fulfilling one.

Community and Philanthropic Goals

If we take another step outwards and go beyond family, it is giving something to the community.

This is where you evoke your aspirations for involving with your community and being a philanthropist.

For example, your way to give to the community could be by building a scholarship fund or supporting your favorite local charity.

You can also volunteer regularly so that you can support causes that matter to you and align with your values. Plus, you get to connect and build warm relationships with the community as a result.

When you determine charity and other philanthropic contributions as part of your legacy plan, this will automatically reflect in your estate plan to maximize its effectiveness.

Once you have defined your legacy by assessing the three key areas, you can then plan to communicate it.

Communicating Your Legacy

Defining your legacy is usually the easiest step out of what we will learn in this chapter.

Communicating your legacy is a necessary step and it requires being transparent and expressive with your voice.

Here are a few effective ways in which you can communicate your legacy to your loved ones and the people around you whom you dearly care about:

Family Meetings

Sharing your legacy plan with your family should be on top of your priorities list. One smooth method you can use is to hold regular family meetings.

Schedule family meetings at least once a month or once every year in case everyone is settled in foreign states or countries.

The agenda of a family meeting should be to discuss your estate plan, and legacy goals, and also articulate the values you wish to pass on.

This not only helps you to communicate your deepest personal thoughts to your family but also allows questions from family members to ensure they understand your plans and are aligned with your wishes.

Ethical Wills

Family meetings are a recurring strategy that you can keep to communicate your legacy. If you want to communicate your legacy in writing, then this is where an ethical will can help you.

Ethical wills are different from your regular wills. The key characteristics of ethical wills are that they provide non-material wisdom and memories, and add a personal tone to your message.

Regular wills are legal documents that instruct the distribution of money or property. Whereas, an ethical will is like a personal gift that you leave behind for your loved ones.

Writing an ethical will is not to talk about assets or intensify grievances. It is a note that you leave behind to lift spirits and leave a powerful mark on your loved one's hearts.

You can share various things in an ethical will, such as your values, experiences, beliefs, and most importantly memories that you shared with your family.

You can include photographs, diary notes, and any additional document that helps to recall memorable moments.

Storytelling and Memory Sharing

Writing an ethical will, combined with perfect storytelling, helps to communicate your legacy as you intend to.

Storytelling is a powerful aspect one can use to share significant family memories and life lessons. People remember and recall stories better than just plain written facts. Moreover, stories help to reinforce values and strengthen your family bonds.

Sharing stories may vary from individual to individual. You could be a successful entrepreneur who can share stories of a family business or how you built the business from scratch to inspire future generations.

You could be a successful doctor who has dedicated a portion of one's life to treating and saving the lives of patients. You can share stories of events that shaped you as a professional and what your heirs can learn about life and helping people.

Anyone can find their own story and memory to share that can instantly impact the hearts of many. In his book *Storyworthy,* Mathew Dicks shares an important exercise one can implement instantly in their lives and see that they have a life made of memorable stories (Dicks, 2018).

He calls it "Homework for Life" where each day, you record something memorable that happened and save it in a book or spreadsheet.

Doing this daily can help you store your precious stories in one safe place and recall them when you read out some of the words you wrote about them. You will be amazed to find out that your life consists of a lot of stories.

Even if you feel you are too old to start doing this, start doing it today and you will still be able to get a few memorable stories to share that align with your values and communicate important life lessons.

Sharing memories by telling stories can tell a lot more about the person than the story itself. When you communicate your legacy with storytelling, lean towards focusing on sharing the most important or life-changing moments in your life.

I even encourage you to start your stories by sharing difficulties and sometimes sad moments in your life that you endured and eventually, overcame. This can leave a huge impact on your heirs and future generations who view positive transformation as an inspiration. We all love such transformational stories!

It doesn't matter if generations below you may not relate to certain things such as the time that you never had a smartphone, or had to walk a few miles to get public transport. The main thing is they can resonate with your emotions and feelings of how you endured one point in your life and how you overcame it to where you are today.

Maintain a positive tone of your stories or what you leave in your ethical will by recalling the happiest moments in life you shared with your family.

This could be that one family trip that you could not forget about or the day you stared at your newborn child's eyes for the first time. It could be even the simplest of things that happen every year, like the Christmas or Thanksgiving dinner you spend with them.

Navigating Family Dynamics

Defining and communicating your legacy is something you do at the surface level.

The last and another integral part that defines your legacy plan is your ongoing actions. And what better way to put in those actions and that is by navigating family dynamics.

People will remember you better for your actions rather than words. Though words can be powerful, your actions stay longer with your loved ones.

Here are a few things you can do that can help you navigate your family situation better.

Addressing Conflicts

Unfortunately, the price that comes with estate planning can often arise from potential family conflicts.

Be proactive and address these potential conflicts as soon as possible. Don't allow the negative atmosphere to reside and end up consuming your entire family. It should be dealt with immediately.

One common family conflict that usually arises is when heirs have differing expectations from the estate plan you created. This is where transparency is vital whenever you create or update your estate plan—especially being transparent to your loved ones.

Be honest and provide reasons behind your decisions so that no one is kept in the dark and any potential misunderstandings can be cleared.

Fairness vs. Equality

Besides addressing potential conflicts, understanding your love and respect towards your family defines you as a parent, grandparent, or sibling.

There is a fine line between being fair and equal. Treating heirs fairly should be prioritized more rather than treating them equally. This may sound controversial at first but hear me out.

Many estate planners make a huge error because they treat their heirs and beneficiaries *equally*, sometimes way too much that it may not reflect how they really want to help some of their family members.

For instance, one should prioritize providing more for a child who requires special needs than a child who has been successful and has financial resources to support themselves.

You have to assess family dynamics and ask yourself, how you can be fair to each family member as much as possible, without disrespecting them. Your legacy can be defined by that.

Preparing the Next Generation

Earlier I mentioned my friend being a long-term visionary and setting aside education funds for future generations. He had the desire to prepare the next generation of his bloodline to preserve valuable family traditions and life values.

Educating and involving the next generation in estate planning or even legacy discussions can be a good way to prepare them for their foreseeable future.

They can learn important traits and lessons from you such as being involved in making the community better through philanthropic initiatives or even preserving some of the family's rich traditions and values.

A legacy plan adds your personal touch and communicates what you experienced in life and what you hope for future generations.

It can be emotional when one assembles memories, stories, photographs, and so on, but it is the most fulfilling and worthy thing to do to reflect on a memorable life that you can be proud of.

As we conclude, let's reflect on this incredible journey and the peace of mind you have achieved.

Bonus Chapter:

Estate Planning as a Lifelong Process

Before concluding this book, I would like to cover something more in this bonus chapter—the importance of incorporating estate planning as a lifelong process.

Estate planning is like a beautiful garden that needs tending regularly.

So far, you have acquired a lot of knowledge that you can use to create your estate plan. You can start working on the front foot and successfully create one.

But doing this process again and again during your lifetime can have a huge impact on your decision to shape your life and your family's.

Being involved in estate planning is expected to be a dynamic and lifelong journey.

This final chapter will emphasize the importance of adapting one's plan to life changes, continuously learning, and engaging with the community to keep an estate plan relevant and effective.

The Evolving Nature of Estate Planning

Your estate plan will naturally evolve with time. You cannot avoid or ignore this.

Since life is dynamic and evolves with time, so this would instantly mean that your estate plan would.

Below are three methods in which you can stay flexible and adapt to the dynamic nature of your estate plan:

Life Stages and Estate Planning

The first and easiest step you can take to evolve your estate plan is to recognize the need to change it at various life stages.

Everyone goes through different phases in their life. This could be being single in their adulthood, marrying the love of their life, being a parent, and even life after retirement is a phase in itself.

When you encounter each different life stage, immediately recognize the need for changing and updating your estate plan so it stays relevant to your life situation.

You may create an estate plan when you are 40 years old. At that time, you could be still growing your financial wealth, and taking care of your children. One detail you prioritize on your estate plan could be assigning limited assets for your children when they grow up.

Now, picture your situation, 20 years later. You are 60 years old. By that time, you might have fully retired, and established more financial resources around you, and your children might have got married and are expecting their first child.

Suddenly, the whole situation changes and the need to update your estate plan becomes a certainty. For instance, you would have more assets to give to your children and now your grandchildren.

Moreover, you would have become wiser to include more important estate planning goals that make you think about future generations and beyond.

This is natural in life and your estate plan should reflect that.

Adapting to Personal and Financial Growth

As explained in the previous example, changes in your personal and financial growth gave you the urge to adapt your estate plan according to those circumstances.

Over time and when things go well, you can see your career advancing and your wealth increasing. This also evolves your estate plan into a more effective and efficient plan.

With more assets, your estate plan requires you to adopt better and more effective ways to manage and navigate the complexities of such assets.

Additionally, it may raise tax implications that require you to address or even legacy goals that you feel will leave a powerful impression on this world.

For comparison, you can relate an estate plan with a human muscle. Your evolving life situation can create more complexities (for the right reasons) and this can challenge your estate plan.

It breaks down pre-existing provisions and instructs it to create newer and stronger provisions that are aligned to your current life situation, just like how a muscle would.

Anticipating Future Needs

Not only you should wait for changes to happen in the future but stay prepared for them. Being proactive in anticipating future needs is a great intuitive skill one can possess.

Your estate plan may require you to proactively plan for such future needs. This can include planning for retirement, healthcare needs, and potential long-term care.

Assessing such future needs helps make forthcoming plans for your estate plan. But most importantly, it helps you to reassess your current personal and financial situation, and establish goals that can help you improve your circumstances and aim higher.

Continuous Education and Awareness

An estate plan requires adapting to your life situation. But in the end, you have to understand that only YOU can make that change.

Your estate planning attorney, financial advisors, accountants, therapists, and even your close family members can't help you with that. You know your life is the best out of everyone I mentioned.

So, this means you are the one who should initiate changes and the best way to do that is to continuously educate yourself and be aware of the world around you.

Keeping Informed on Legal Changes

Staying informed about legal changes can be a tricky task. If you can stay ahead of changes in estate-related laws such as tax laws, probate procedures, etc., then consider yourself a few steps ahead in the game.

Laws can change more frequently than you imagine. This is why I stressed the need to maintain a network of professionals around you so that you can continuously get updated on any significant changes in estate laws.

Being informed of such changes can help you to adapt your estate strategy to maintain its full effectiveness and comply with relevant and up-to-date regulations. As a result, you maintain your estate plan in the way you want and *legally*.

One common example is how a new tax law might urge you to revise your asset allocation and distribution strategy so that you can keep maximizing tax benefits along the way.

Staying Updated with Financial Trends

Apart from legal changes, staying updated with financial trends is a must as well.

Financial markets can impact your assets and investments. As a result, this impacts your estate plan.

Monitor financial markets regularly and even identify potential investment opportunities that can help you grow your estate and also protect it.

For instance, cryptocurrency is something for the future. If you invest in that now and make it a part of your investments, you are leaving future generations with a valuable asset that is *relevant* to their generation and can benefit them massively.

Lifelong Learning in Estate Planning

When you commit to ongoing education in understanding more estate planning principles and strategies, this can help you massively in your estate planning over time.

Your knowledge should not only be limited to just a few resources. Embrace the potential of the internet and also learn from others who have done their estate planning to learn a few things that can help with your estate plan.

You can acquire knowledge from various sources. Reading more books, taking on more online courses, or consultations with estate planning professionals.

Either way, it is going to expand your thinking and make you understand the application of effective estate planning practices.

Engaging with Estate Planning Communities

I know it can be difficult to implement actions in isolation and expect to do them every time.

You have important things to think about and do daily in your life, and sometimes just going through the stress of reading more books or online courses can be challenging.

This is why I like to build systems around my daily routine that create accountability and passively provide me with adequate knowledge to stay updated with estate planning laws and current affairs.

The following are some effective ways in which you can build systems that will continuously provide you with knowledge without you proactively seeking it:

Joining Support Groups and Forums

Nowadays, you see online groups and forums being a major source of acquiring relevant and updated information.

When you participate in support groups or online forums related to estate planning, it can help you for different purposes.

Firstly, you will get to find congregations where you can openly share experiences that you encountered in your estate planning journey.

Secondly, you get to find emotional support from like-minded people during your planning process. Thirdly, you acquire new information that you may have never learned about before and this can benefit your estate plan.

Lastly, you get to help others just like you work on their estate plan and create warm connections.

Join groups or forums that are specially tailored and *relevant to your needs*.

For example, if you are a parent who has a child who requires special needs, then join a similar forum with parents of special needs children.

This helps to provide valuable and relevant advice on various things such as how to set up a special needs trust, how to optimize your legacy plan, and so on.

Attending Workshops and Seminars

When online courses may require some work and discipline from your side, workshops and seminars are the more relaxed options.

Not only workshops and seminars are usually conducted in one sitting but also package important and relevant information into one session. It removes the fluff and only provides you with information on what matters to your estate planning needs.

Workshops and seminars are nowadays a way that professionals use as part of their marketing strategy to promote products and services.

You might get lucky to attend a workshop or seminar of a top estate planning attorney who gave you upfront value. This can help you connect with them and have someone who can help you with your estate plan for life. Hence, take advantage of it.

Networking with Professionals and Peers

Finally, your network with peers and professionals completes your system. Focus on building a network of estate planning professionals who offer valuable advice, referrals, and support.

As I mentioned earlier, when you engage with a community of like-minded people, it can provide more opportunities for you to learn new things and optimize your estate planning efforts.

You must prioritize the collaboration of such professionals or peers so that you can constantly stay updated on various estate-related news and use their expertise to your advantage.

You have learned to embrace estate planning as a lifelong journey. It is time to wrap up everything we have learned!

Conclusion

The more informed we are, the more we understand and the better we're able to protect ourselves, our family, and assets. —
Spencer Sean (Tom, 2023)

As we conclude the book, I will leave you with some parting words of wisdom as you embark on your journey to create and maintain an effective estate plan.

An estate plan that not only shows how you want to distribute your assets but a plan that showcases your legacy!

You started with learning the basics of estate planning. Thus, understanding the need for it.

The first step towards effective estate planning is assessing your needs and goals.

Then, you start setting up and including important estate planning documents: your will, trusts, advanced healthcare directives, and powers of attorney.

Take more measures to protect and preserve your assets for your family and other beneficiaries. And finally, minimize tax liability by optimizing your tax planning.

These steps you have learned will help you take off your estate plan more easily than you initially thought. And remember WHY you are doing this: To ensure your family gets the inheritance they deserve and also to ensure there are fewer complications and potential conflicts after you pass away. Creating an estate plan solves that.

But wait! Your obligation to your estate plan doesn't end there. You must continuously review and update your plan so it stays relevant to your life circumstances and guides you toward evolving into a more robust plan.

A legacy plan helps personally communicate your values and share inspiring stories that define you as a person and the memories you shared with your loved ones.

This book itself should be used like how you would need to keep reviewing your estate plan. Use it as a guide so that you can read it multiple times to get the most value out of it.

Empowerment comes from taking a proactive approach to fulfilling your estate planning goals. You are the hero of your story—a story that shapes your legacy and secures your family's bright future.

I thank you for taking the time to complete reading this book.

As someone who knows the importance of estate planning, I encourage you to regularly review and update your estate plans to reflect your current circumstances, goals, and major developments.

Make estate planning a priority from today!

If you got value out of this book, please leave a review so that other devoted fathers and mothers just like you can build their estate plans and secure their families' futures.

So, don't leave your estate planning hanging any longer. Take your first step today and establish your estate planning needs and goals.

I wish you and your family the best! They are counting on you!

Glossary

AB Trust: A type of trust that married couples make use of for tax purposes. It is split into two trusts—the A trust contains the estate of the survivor spouse, whereas the B trust contains the estate of the deceased.

Administration: Refers to the procedure of overseeing the management and distribution of the deceased's estate in a court-supervised manner.

Administrator: For intestate individuals, the probate court appoints an administrator to manage the distribution of the deceased's estate.

Annuity: A fixed sum of money that is paid periodically or for life depending on the established agreement.

Appraise: Utilizing an authorized individual to value or estimate the value of assets or properties.

Asset Allocation: An investment strategy that works by dividing investments among various kinds of asset classes.

Beneficiary: A person who has been named by the testator, grantor, or policyholder to receive benefits from a will, trust, or insurance policy.

Bequest: Refers to a gift left to someone in a will.

Buy-Sell Agreement: A contractual agreement that closely-held businesses utilize to allow existing partners to acquire shares of their deceased partner.

Charitable Lead Trust: A charitable trust that provides income to charities during the grantor's lifetime, after which the remaining assets will be distributed to the grantor and other beneficiaries.

Charitable Remainder Trust: A charitable trust that provides annuities to the grantor during their lifetime, after which the remaining assets are donated to charity.

Closely-Held Business: A type of business ownership structure that has limited number of partners, specifically coming from the same family.

Codicil: An amendment to a will that outlines what provisions to alter or revoke in a will.

Community Property State: These are states that have assets jointly-owned by spouses during their marriage.

Conservator: An individual whom the court appoints to control and protect the estate of a person due to their age, mental capacity, health, etc.

Contest: This refers to someone challenging the provisions stated in the testator's will as a way to gain more from their estate.

Creditor: Can be a person or institution to whom money is owed and should be paid.

Custodial Account: An account that makes it possible to gift assets or facilitate trust distributions to minors under the age of 18 or 21.

Decedent: Refers to a person who has died.

Deed- A legal agreement that enables to transfer of title of real estate property under the law.

Descendants- Refers to the individual's children, grandchildren, and other people related by blood or legal adoption.

Disinherit: To prevent someone from inheriting an asset or estate.

Distribution: Refers to the procedure of giving away all of the assets, properties, or inheritance to beneficiaries during an estate settlement.

Durable Power of Attorney: A power of attorney that does not end upon the person who made the power of attorney's incapacity.

Estate: An estate of a deceased refers to the total assets they own and liabilities they owe.

Estate Freeze: A type of strategy that is employed to lock in the current value of an estate, mainly done for tax purposes.

Estate Tax: These taxes are levied on an individual's property and assets after their death.

Executor: The person who is appointed by the testator of a will to administer their estate after the testator passes away.

Fiduciary: Typically refers to a personal representative, trustee, or guardian, as someone who takes care and manages money or assets for someone else.

Generation-Skipping Transfer Tax (GSTT): Taxes levied on the assets transferred to a generation below the next generation, fundamentally, skipping a generation to transfer wealth.

Gift: A monetary or materialistic transfer from one person to another without any compensation in return.

Guardianship: It refers to the legal responsibility for caring for someone who can't manage affairs on their own, typically minors or adults who lack mental capacity.

Healthcare Power of Attorney: An individual who is designated to make healthcare decisions on behalf of the person who made the power of attorney.

Heir: Refers to an individual who is entitled to a distribution of one's estate such as assets or properties under respective state laws. Heirs are different from beneficiaries.

Holographic Will: A will that doesn't need to be witnessed as the content and signature are in the testator's handwriting.

Incapacity: Refers to the situation or circumstance where a person is unable to act or make decisions by themself.

Inherit: The act of receiving an asset or property from a deceased individual.

Inheritance Tax: Taxes levied on beneficiaries after they inherit something.

Insurance Trust: An irrevocable trust where one can transfer insurance policies and the proceedings will go to their beneficiaries.

Inter Vivos Trust: A name given to a living trust, where the trust is set up during the grantor's lifetime.

Intestate: The condition or circumstance of someone dying without a valid will.

Irrevocable: A type of trust in which the trustor has given up the right to modify, alter, or terminate the trust once it is created.

Joint Tenancy: When two or more people hold interests in the same property with the right of survivorship, it is said to have co-ownership or joint tenancy.

Life Estate: When an individual has the rights to use the property or asset only during their lifetime.

Living Trust: A type of trust that's established during the trustor's lifetime.

Living Will: A legal document or instrument that outlines a person's wishes concerning their medical treatment if they become incapacitated.

Marital Deduction: A federal tax code provision that allows one spouse to transfer unlimited assets to the other spouse tax-free.

Marital Trust: A trust that is meant for couples where the deceased spouse can hold assets for a surviving spouse, and it is designed for marital deductions.

Minor: A minor is a person who has not reached the legal age. This can be 18 or 21 years of age depending on some states.

No-Contest Clause: A particular provision included in a will or trust that ensures the one who challenges the will for the benefit of getting more from the estate, will lose any inheritance rights they have.

Pay on Death (POD): Established between a bank and an account holder to transfer their assets to the beneficiaries after the account holder's death.

Pour-Over Will: A will that allows any assets that are not covered in a will to be transferred to a trust after the grantor's death.

Power of Attorney: A legal authority granted to a person to make financial or healthcare decisions on behalf of another person.

Probate: A legal court process where the will of the deceased person is validated and the distribution of their assets.

Probate Fees: Includes fees that are processed and paid during a probate court process, such as court legal and administrative fees, executor fees, and other expenses.

Physician Orders for Life-Sustaining Treatment (POLST): A form that once it is signed, can be used to authorize the patient to control their medical treatments till death.

Residuary Estate: Once the estate settles its debts, pays taxes, and distributes assets to its beneficiaries, the remainder of it is said to be the residuary estate.

Revocable: This is a type of trust that once created by the trustor, still holds rights to modify, alter, or terminate the trust during their lifetime.

Separate Property: Refers to a property that is bought, gifted, or even inherited before a person's marriage.

Settle an Estate: The legal procedure of evaluating the deceased person's assets, paying debt and taxes, and finally distributing all the assets to their beneficiaries.

Spendthrift Trust: A trust that allows a person to distribute assets to their beneficiaries over time, rather than all at once.

Successor Trustee: A person who succeeds or takes over as the trustee of a trust after the primary trustee resigns or passes away.

Surviving Spouse: A spouse who outlives their other spouse by a minimum of 120 hours.

Testamentary Trust: Unlike a living trust, this type of trust is established or becomes effective after the testator's death as instructed in their will. Testamentary trusts must go through probate.

Testator: Refers to the person who originally created a will.

Title: A title refers to a legal ownership of a real estate property or other types of assets.

Transfer on Death (TOD): Designing funds, assets, or securities to beneficiaries and only transferred upon the death of the account holder.

Transfer Tax: It is the tax levied on assets transferred from one person to another.

Trust: It is the legal relationship created by one party (known as the trustor) who grants legal rights to a trustee to own assets, for the benefit of providing the trustor's beneficiaries.

Trustee: The person or corporate entity who is appointed to manage the assets within the trust and distribute them to all beneficiaries.

Trustor: Referred to the maker of the trust, they can also be referred to as a grantor or settlor.

Will: It is a legal instrument that outlays a person's wishes and directions to distribute their assets or properties after their death.

Witness: Refers to a person who watches the legal signing of a will or other estate-related documents.

References

Charitable lead trust or charitable remainder trust? | Truist. (2024). Truist. https://www.truist.com/resources/wealth/articles/charitable-lead-trust-or-charitable-remainder-trust

Dicks, M. (2018). *Storyworthy.* New World Library.

Digital Estate Planning: How To Organize All Your Digital Property and Assets. (n.d.). Www.everplans.com. https://www.everplans.com/articles/digital-estate-planning-how-to-organize-all-your-digital-property-and-assets

Do Not Become a Statistic: Estate Planning Is Important for Everyone. (n.d.). *Squillace & Associates, P.C.* https://squillace-law.com/do-not-become-a-statistic-estate-planning-is-important-for-everyone/

Durable (Financial) and General Powers of Attorney: Compared. (2020, December 28). EForms Learn. https://learn.eforms.com/estate-planning/durable-financial-and-general-power-of-attorney-comparison/

Estate Planning Guide and Checklist (2023) | NCOA.org. (n.d.). National Council on Aging. https://www.ncoa.org/adviser/estate-planning/estate-planning-guide-checklist/

Estate Planning vs. Will: What's the Difference? (2022, July 6). SmartAsset. https://smartasset.com/estate-planning/estate-planning-vs-will

Estate Tax: Definition, Tax Rates and Who Pays in 2020-2021. (n.d.). NerdWallet. https://www.nerdwallet.com/article/taxes/estate-tax

Estate tax vs. inheritance tax: Who pays & in which states? (2022, December 1). Thrivent.com. https://www.thrivent.com/insights/estate-planning/estate-tax-vs-inheritance-tax-who-pays-and-in-which-states

Financial Power of Attorney - Role and Responsibilities. (n.d.). Trust & Will. https://trustandwill.com/learn/financial-power-of-attorney

Five Key Elements of an Estate Plan – Ahead of the Curve Law. (n.d.). https://aheadofthecurvelaw.com/2017/11/08/five-key-elements-of-an-estate-plan/

4 Common Types of Trusts Compared (Pros & Cons). (n.d.). Trustpointinc.com. https://trustpointinc.com/types-of-trusts-compared-pros-cons/

4 Estate Planning Strategies to Protect Your Assets. (2022, May 19). New York Estate Planning & Elder Law Blog. https://www.trustlaw.com/blog/4-estate-planning-strategies-to-protect-your-assets-2/

Haley, R. W. (2023, November 20). *Maximizing Your Legacy: Strategic Ways to Include Charities in Your Estate Plan.* The Estate & Elder Law Center of Southside Virginia, PLLC. https://vaelderlaw.com/strategic-ways-to-include-charities-in-your-estate-plan/

Harton, O. (2023, September 6). *10 Ways to Reduce Estate Taxes*. Findlaw. https://www.findlaw.com/estate/planning-an-estate/10-ways-to-reduce-estate-taxes.html

How do I create a will? Your estate planning guide. (n.d.). Www.legalzoom.com. https://www.legalzoom.com/articles/how-do-i-create-a-will/

Inheritance Tax: Who Pays & Which States in 2021-2022. (n.d.). NerdWallet. https://www.nerdwallet.com/article/taxes/inheritance-tax

Inheritance tax vs estate tax. (n.d.). Protective.com. https://www.protective.com/learn/what-is-the-difference-between-inheritance-tax-and-estate-tax

Instructions for Form 706 | Internal Revenue Service. (2018). Irs.gov. https://www.irs.gov/instructions/i706

Kagan, J. (2019). *Estate planning*. Investopedia. https://www.investopedia.com/terms/e/estateplanning.asp

Living Wills and Advance Health Care Directives Under the Law. (2021, March 16). Justia. https://www.justia.com/estate-planning/wills/living-wills-advance-health-care-directives/

Macnaught, L. (2018, December 10). *The Special Needs Trust: 3 Types*. Synergy. https://synergysettlements.com/the-special-needs-trust-3-types/

Preparing a Living Will. (n.d.). National Institute on Aging. https://www.nia.nih.gov/health/advance-care-planning/preparing-living-will

Priyanka Prakash, JD. (2018, September 14). *Estate Planning for Small Business Owners in 8 Steps*. Fundera.com; Fundera. https://www.fundera.com/blog/estate-planning-for-small-business-owners

Procedure for making advance directive; notice to physician. (2024). Virginia.gov. https://law.lis.virginia.gov/vacode/title54.1/chapter29/section54.1-2983/

Rubin, H. (2021, April 30). *Financial vs. Medical Power of Attorney: What's the Difference?* Investopedia. https://www.investopedia.com/articles/managing-wealth/042216/medical-vs-financial-power-attorney-reasons-separate-them.asp

6 tips to help minimize estate taxes | Why everyone needs an estate plan| Fidelity. (2023, March 1). Www.fidelity.com. https://www.fidelity.com/learning-center/personal-finance/how-to-avoid-estate-taxes

State Death Tax Chart. (n.d.). The American College of Trust and Estate Counsel. https://www.actec.org/resources-for-wealth-planning-professionals/state-death-tax-chart/

Sweatt, L. (2016, December 8). *11 Quotes About Leaving a Legacy | SUCCESS*. SUCCESS. https://www.success.com/11-quotes-about-leaving-a-legacy/

10 Common Estate Planning Mistakes (and How to Avoid Them). (n.d.). Kiplinger. https://www.kiplinger.com/slideshow/retirement/t021-s014-10-common-estate-planning-mistakes-to-avoid/index.html

The Difference Between Durable and Springing Power of Attorney. (2022, June 30). Herold Law, P.A. https://www.heroldlaw.com/blog/2022/06/difference-between-durable-springing-power-of-attorney/

The Top 7 Estate Planning Objectives. (2020, June 22). U of I Tax School. https://taxschool.illinois.edu/post/the-top-7-estate-planning-objectives/

3 Common Mistakes to Avoid with Your Power of Attorney. (2019, October 20). Solan, Park & Robello. https://solanpark.com/3-common-mistakes-to-avoid-with-your-power-of-attorney/

Tips and Advice on Estate Planning for Blended Families. (n.d.). Trust & Will. https://trustandwill.com/learn/estate-planning-for-blended-families

Tom. (2023, September 19). *12 Inspirational Quotes About Estate Planning.* Leigh Hilton. https://dentonestateplanninglawyer.com/12-inspirational-quotes-about-estate-planning/

Trusts: Definition, Types, Purposes & Benefits. (2023, August 1). NerdWallet. https://www.nerdwallet.com/article/investing/estate-planning/setting-up-a-trust

Types of Trusts - Which Option is Right for You. (n.d.). Trust & Will. https://trustandwill.com/learn/types-of-trusts

Understanding the basics of estate planning. (n.d.). https://personal1.vanguard.com/pdf/a129.pdf

What Are Inheritance Taxes? (n.d.). Turbotax.intuit.com. https://turbotax.intuit.com/tax-tips/estates/what-are-inheritance-taxes/L93IUc3sC

What is an Ethical Will and What is It Used For? (n.d.). Trust & Will. https://trustandwill.com/learn/ethical-will

What Is Included in an Estate Inventory? - SmartAsset. (n.d.). Smartasset.com. https://smartasset.com/estate-planning/what-is-included-in-an-estate-inventory

Will(ful) Neglect: Survey Reveals Nearly 60% of Americans Unprepared for the Inevitable. (2023, August 8). Businesswire. https://www.businesswire.com/news/home/20230808403417/en/

Yokabitus, P. (2019, April 17). *The 4 D's of Reviewing Your Estate Plan | Planning for Any Circumstance.* Cary Estate Planning. https://caryestateplanning.com/blog/the-4-ds-of-reviewing-your-estate-plan/

Your guide to living wills and other advance directives. (2022, August 2). Mayo Clinic. https://www.mayoclinic.org/healthy-lifestyle/consumer-health/in-depth/living-wills/art-20046303

www.ingramcontent.com/pod-product-compliance
Lightning Source LLC
Chambersburg PA
CBHW062224220526
45471CB00009B/3333